WHAT'S YOUR ASTITVA?

Celebrating Diversity in Different Identities

AF516788

WHAT'S YOUR ASTITVA?

Celebrating Diversity in Different Identities

By Astitva Teens Team

EXCELLER BOOKS®
A GLOBAL PRESS

WHAT'S YOUR ASTITVA

Celebrating Diversity in Different Identities

Copyright © Sheryl Tayal, India, 2025

Cover by Exceller Books

All rights reserved. No portion of the book may or should be reproduced, stored in any retrieval system (including but not limited to computers, disks, external drives, electronic or digital devices, e-readers, websites), or transmitted in any form or by any means (mechanical, recording, electronic, digital version, photocopying, or otherwise) without the prior, written permission of the publisher, nor be otherwise circulated in any form of binding or cover other than that in which it is published and without a similar condition being imposed on the subsequent purchaser.

The book has been published with all reasonable efforts taken to make the material error-free after the consent of the authors. The views and opinions expressed in this book are the authors' own and the facts are as reported by them. Neither the publisher nor editor endorse or approve the content of this book or guaranty the reliability, accuracy or completeness of the content published herein and do not make and representations of warranties of any kind, express or implied, including but not limited to the implied warranties of merchantability, fitness for a particular purpose. The publisher or editor shall not be liable whatsoever for any errors, omissions, whether such errors or omissions result from negligence, accident or any other cause or claims for loss or damage of any kind, including without limitation damage arising out of use, or about reliability, accuracy, sufficiency of the information contained in this book.

ISBN: 978-93-48892-44-7

First published in India in 2025 by Exceller Books,

An imprint of GE Group

G1, Dream Apartment, Degree College Road, Belgharia,

Kolkata, 700056, India

www.excellerbooks.com

EXCELLER BOOKS®

A GLOBAL PRESS

Contents

–Introduction to Astitva Teens– Celebrating Diversity in Different Identities

Astitva Teens is a non-profit organization that works towards educating teens about identities and the LGBTQIA+ community to create safe and inclusive spaces within school.

Here is the door— a door to freedom, to dreams untamed. A passage leading you to heights you've never dared to explore. A door you'd adore, not for what it is, but for what it opens...

Une porte. Una Puerta

It doesn't just swing open. It beckons, it pulls, it dares. Step through and you will find yourself into a space that almost feels unreal, a utopia dancing on the edge of imagination, where possibility is not a distant whisper but a voice standing strong.

But tell me, who builds the world? Who gives it shape, its breath, its pulse?

We do. It's us. Always us.

We are the ones who will tear down the heavy, rusted pillars of a patriarchal past, smashing the weight of orthodox and rebuild something— something real, something luminous. Something that doesn't just exist but thrives.

A society not carved from sameness but sculpted by distinguished diversity, where what makes you "YOU" is the foundation that is not tolerated- it is celebrated. Whether you're gay, lesbian, trans, asexual, non-binary or straight, it doesn't matter.

You matter. What matters is you, your heart, your art, your voice. That's what will echo in this new world.

Here, you won't get just equality; you'll get equity. The kind that listens to your story, sees your scars, and still says, "Come as you are."

Your struggles won't be brushed aside like dust on a crowed street, with a careless hand. They'll be felt. Shared. Embraced.

And those layers of yours— those intersecting, complex, beautiful layers— will find warmth here, not rejection.

This world? It's not an unreachable dream hanging in the sky. It is real. It is near.

It's not a fantasy hung in some unreachable sky. It's waiting – just a door away. Waiting for us to grow into the kind of humans who don't just walk but rise.

A world that belongs to all of us – yours, mines and everyone's. A world that does not wait for permission to change. A world that takes shape when we rise, when we dare to take charge, in schools where young minds learn, in offices where decision takes flight, in every space where change grows roots.

And isn't that what makes us special?

The way we can learn and unlearn, bend and unbend, take the broken pieces and craft something whole again. That's the beauty of us – the way we refuse to be bound by our past. So let me tell you this: you're not alone. You're not the only one dreaming of what could be.

Didn't Lennon once sing about a dream? A world living as one? Well, we're allowed to dream too— big, wild, impossible dreams.

Dreams that don't hover in distance but become real, tangible. Because dreaming alone isn't enough, is it? We must act. We must persist. Build paths, carve ways, and keep walking, step by step, until the world we envision is off this page and into reality.

This door (Book) isn't just a door (Book). This book isn't just words on a page – it's a door. A door that leads to a promise. And when it opens, we won't just stand in its glow—we'll step through it, not as spectators but as creators, as architects of something extraordinary. Something human. Something that finally, finally feels like home.

Part I

The Foundation of Astitva Teens

– Chapter 1 –
About Astitva Teens

How Did It All Begin?

In 2023, I, Sheryl Tayal, the founder of Astitva Teens, witnessed one of my close friends being mistreated when she identified herself as bisexual in front of her school community. The reaction she received was heartbreaking—whispers, judgmental glances, and even outright exclusion. This was not an isolated incident. Over the years, I had seen her endure countless episodes of hate and microaggressions simply because she chose to embrace her true identity. At a tender age of 16, she was already carrying the weight of societal rejection, and this reality jolted me to my core. It made me realize the magnitude of the problem—one that was too vast and too ingrained to just simply ignore.

I remember the evening she confided in me, tears streaming down her face as she recounted the hurtful words and side remarks thrown at her. "Why is it so hard for people to accept me? Am I not enough?" she asked, her voice trembling. I had no answer, and that feeling of helplessness stayed with me. But more than anything, it fuelled a fire within me to act—to ensure that no one else would have to face this kind of rejection alone.

As I began researching, I quickly discovered that acceptance, inclusivity, and respect were among the most pressing issues faced by LGBTQIA+ students. Schools, which should be spaces for safety and learning, were often breeding grounds for intolerance and ignorance. The lack of awareness and empathy was glaring, and I knew that addressing these gaps was not only necessary but also urgent.

Apart from my friend's experience, another stark realization dawned on me during my daily encounters which may be faced by many is transgender individuals at traffic signals, begging for money and food. Every day, I saw them standing there, vulnerable and marginalized by a society that refused to acknowledge them beyond stereotypes. One evening, after a particularly long conversation with my father about this, he explained to me that many of them struggled to find jobs simply because of their identity. This struck a deep chord within me. How can a society that preaches equality deny people their right to livelihood based solely on who they are? Their identity should not affect their skill set!

These moments of pain, injustice, and reflection collectively ignited my journey toward founding *Astitva Teens*. I realized that change begins in schools—where young minds are shaped, where biases can be challenged, and where empathy can be cultivated. If we can initiate conversations early, educate students and teachers alike, and foster an environment that genuinely values diversity, then perhaps the future can be different for those struggling with their identity today.

Starting *Astitva Teens* was not just about launching an initiative—it was about giving a voice to those who had been silenced for too long. It was about standing up for my friend and for every teenager who was feeling alone in their journey of self-discovery. It was about building bridges of understanding and creating safe spaces where every student could express themselves unfiltered, without fear of judgment or exclusion.

The journey has not been easy, but it has been deeply fulfilling. We have a long way to go, but every step we take—every workshop we conduct, every conversation we spark, every policy we advocate for—brings us closer to a world where acceptance is not a privilege but a norm.

Astitva Teens is more than just an organization; it is a movement for change, for awareness, and for the unwavering belief that every individual deserves to be seen, respected, and celebrated for who they truly are—celebrating *diversity in different identities.*

Detailed Background Information about the Organization

Astitva Teens is a youth-led initiative committed to fostering a world where every teenager feels seen, heard, and valued. Our organization focuses on educating teenagers about their identities and the LGBTQIA+ community while creating safe, inclusive, and acceptance-filled spaces within schools. We believe that schools should be environments of understanding, where students are encouraged to embrace their authentic selves without fear of discrimination or exclusion.

At *Astitva Teens,* we recognize the importance of awareness and proactive change in building a culture of acceptance. Through advocacy, education, and community-driven initiatives, we strive to ensure that conversations about identity, diversity, and inclusion become an integral part of the learning experience. By conducting workshops, training sessions, and collaborative discussions, we empower both students and educators to create a more inclusive school environment.

Our work extends beyond awareness—we take tangible steps to bring about social change. We actively collaborate with educators, school administrations, parents, and students to implement policies and programs that promote inclusivity. Whether it is by hosting panel discussions, curating resource materials, or leading student support groups, *Astitva Teens* stands as a guiding force for those seeking a more equitable and compassionate society.

Above all, we believe that actions speak louder than words. We aim not only to initiate conversations but also to inspire meaningful actions that lead to lasting changes in how schools and society at large perceive and support diverse identities.

Our Vision

Our vision is to cultivate a world where every teenager, regardless of their identity, feels safe, accepted, and empowered within their school environment. We strive to create an educational system that normalizes conversations about gender, sexuality, and identity, fostering a culture of respect, inclusivity, and empathy. By breaking down barriers and challenging stereotypes, we aspire to contribute to a generation that embraces diversity as a strength rather than an exception.

Our Mission

Astitva Teens is on a mission to:

- **Educate and Raise Awareness:** Provide accurate, accessible, and inclusive information about gender, sexuality, and identity to students, educators, and parents.

- **Create Safe Spaces:** Establish school environments where teenagers feel comfortable expressing themselves without fear of judgment, discrimination, or isolation.
- **Encourage Allyship and Community Building:** Promote allyship by educating peers on how they can support and uplift LGBTQIA+ individuals in meaningful and respectful ways.
- **Empower and Support Teenagers:** Equip young individuals with the knowledge, confidence, and resources to advocate for their rights and the rights of others.
- **Train Educators and School Leaders:** Develop training programs that help teachers and school administrators foster an inclusive learning environment.
- **Advocate for Policy Changes:** Work towards the inclusion of LGBTQIA+ education in school curricula, ensuring that identity-based discrimination is actively addressed.

Through these commitments, *Astitva Teens* continues to work towards an inclusive future where schools are a haven of acceptance, support, and empowerment for all students.

– Chapter 2 –
Introduction of the Contributors

Sheryl Tayal – Founder and CEO (she/her)

"Be yourself; everyone else is already taken." — Oscar Wilde

I am Sheryl Tayal. I am a 16-year-old girl who is not afraid to stand out. I find comfort in fiction—whether through books or television—because stories offer a beautiful escape from reality. *Gilmore Girls* is my all-time favourite show, a world I keep going back to. I am also a die-hard fan of baked goods, whether it is home-baked brownies or the cookies my school offers.

I founded *Astitva Teens* to create a space where students of all ages and diverse identities can come together to take steps that make school a safer and more inclusive environment. I have always been proud of who I am, but there were times when I questioned myself and altered my preferences, demeanour, and even opinions just to fit in. I was trying to balance the need to be true to myself and the desire to belong.

Over time, I realized that embracing my identity, my *Astitva,* was far more important than shrinking to the cookie-cutter mould made by society. That is why I started ***Astitva Teens***—to spread this message, to help others embrace their truth, and to raise awareness about the LGBTQIA+ community.

And if there is one thing I have learned, it is this: self-love is a quiet, unshakable strength.

Geet from *Jab We Met* so perfectly put it, *"Main apni favorite hoon."*

Raaghvi Goel – Chief Writer (She/Her)

"Stories are everywhere, but not all of them are heard."

My name is Raaghvi Goel. I am 15 years old and currently studying in Grade 9. I have always been passionate about writing and reading diverse stories revolving around all walks of life.

In addition, I feel a strong connection with people, animals, and nature, and thus have always had a zeal for the same.

My journey with *Astitva Teens* began when I realized that many stories around me were being told but not truly heard. I wanted to be part of an initiative that amplifies the voices of those who deserve recognition, regardless of race, colour, or gender.

Being part of *Astitva Teens* has presented me with the opportunity to contribute to this cause in a meaningful way by advocating for inclusivity and a more accepting society.

Aanya Gadodia – Supporting writer (she/her)

"We deserve to experience love fully, equally, without shame and without compromise." — Elliot Page

Hi! My name is Aanya Gadodia. I am 14 years old and in 10th grade at Pathways School, Gurgaon. I am a reader, a writer, and passionate about the power of words to spark change.

I have been aware of *Astitva* since its early days, long before it became *Astitva Teens,* an organization dedicated to educating teenagers about identity and the LGBTQIA+ community, while fostering safe, inclusive, and accepting spaces within schools. I officially joined the team as a writer a little while back, driven by the belief that no one should be shunned or discriminated against for simply being who they are.

Humanity thrives on diversity—of race, culture, ethnicity—so why shouldn't identity be part of that spectrum? Why must every individual conform to a predefined perception of "normal," and why should those who do not fit be cast aside? I joined *Astitva Teens* because I believe in making a positive change, and because we will make it right.

Shaza Farooqui – Editor (she/her)

'The jovian plutonian gravitational effect' a phenomenon given by Sir Patrick Moore

A true lover of poetry and literature, music and dance, as well as oceans and mountains, I believe my passion for words and emotions drives me to write poetry - my superpower - and create diverse pieces.

I am the kid who takes cat treats, journals, and books in her bag everywhere. You will find me at bookshops, cafes, and on random streets, feeding cats, and I think that is when I am most myself.

The need to love and share the same idea of love, in all its shapes, sizes, and colours, brought me to *Astitva,* where I saw how closely knit the bonds were within the team. It inculcated a sense of drive and wholesomeness that brought me peace as well.

I have been in *Astitva* for almost a year now, and it has always been a truly fulfilling experience for me. It has shaped me, taught me and helped me grow.

Vidhi Madan – Resource Creator (she/her)

'YOLO - You Only Live Once - is the motto I live by.'

I am Vidhi Madan, a 15-year-old student in the 10th grade. When people jokingly tell me to 'get a hobby,' I wish I could explain that conversing with others is, in fact, my hobby. Connecting with new individuals is what drives me, and I have developed hobbies such as traveling and exploring new restaurants to facilitate these interactions.

This enthusiasm for meeting new people led me to join the *Astitva Teens* team. I saw it as an exciting opportunity to leverage my skills in creating posters and infographics. As someone who appreciates creativity, I am fascinated by the way people express themselves through art. I believe that creative expression reveals a lot about a person's thoughts and psychology.

My ultimate goal in life is happiness, and I make conscious choices that align with achieving it. *Astitva Teens* gave me the opportunity to pursue this goal while doing something I love. I am thrilled to be part of this team and look forward to continuing to work with it in the future.

Riddhi Singh – Resource Creator (she/her)

"When the whole world is silent, even one voice becomes powerful."
— Malala Yousafzai

I am Riddhi, and I am 13 years old. I enjoy playing basketball and interacting with my friends. I am quite an extrovert, and talking to people drives me. I enjoy cooking a wide range of dishes, from pasta to baked goods.

I am a true believer in *Astitva Teens'* vision and mission. I joined *Astitva Teens* because I believe everyone deserves a space where they feel safe, accepted, and free to be themselves—no matter their gender identity or sexual orientation.

I enjoyed creating infographics and have developed skills in graphic design, so I decided to join the team and have grown significantly since then.

I am passionate about understanding different perspectives and making the world a kinder place. Being part of *Astitva Teens* gives me the opportunity to learn, raise awareness, and be part of a movement that is actually making a difference.

Other Contributors

- **Creative Expression, Poet**: Medha Matta, a 15-year-old student at Pathways School, Gurgaon, is passionate about writing and an opinionated soul who believes in standing up for others' rights.
- **Poet and Writer**: Arshan has been part of the *Astitva Teens* team since its inception and has contributed blogs and poems to this book.
- **Writer**: Vidhi Singhal, a 13-year-old student at Pathways School, Gurgaon, supports the LGBTQIA+ community and advocates for their rights.

- **Researcher:** Kiyansh Khurana, a 13-year-old student at Pathways School, Gurgaon, believes that everyone should have a space where they can be themselves without fear of judgement.

Astitva Teens Voice, Writer: Ms Sonia Bambi Seth, a Chief Life Designer and Spiritual Healer, embodies the true value of "I am enough" and believes that self-love and acceptance come from within.

Part II
Astitva Teens Initiatives and Voices

– Chapter 3 –
Initiatives & Programs

Astitva Teens Initiatives

Astitva Teens: A Journey of Advocacy, Awareness, and Action

Astitva Teens was founded through an inter-school panel discussion organized at Pathways School, Gurgaon, in February 2024. This event aimed to break stereotypes, initiate meaningful conversations, and foster inclusivity within schools. Schools from across Delhi NCR, including various IB institutions, were invited to participate. The panel featured distinguished professionals from diverse fields, all of whom have made significant contributions to the LGBTQIA+ rights movement and advocacy. The discussion focused on creating awareness, challenging societal norms, and encouraging dialogue within school communities.

In addition to the panel discussion, a student exhibition was organized to provide a platform for artistic and literary expressions on themes related to identity, inclusion, and self-expression. This exhibition allowed students to

showcase their work through various media, ensuring that their voices were acknowledged and celebrated. The event drew an attendance of over 150 students, parents, and educators, reflecting the growing interest in fostering a more inclusive school environment.

Festival of Hope: Moving from Discussion to Action

Building on the success of the panel discussion, *Astitva Teens* organized a second event, part of the Festival of Hope, at Pathways School in Gurgaon, scheduled for September 26, 2024. Unlike the previous event, which focused on discussion, this initiative focused on taking actionable steps towards inclusivity and raising awareness. The event included an identity session conducted by a counselor, during which students explored themes of emotional regulation, personal feelings, and bullying in a safe and open environment.

A significant part of the event consisted of interactive workshops led by LGBTQIA+ professionals, designed to equip

students with the skills and tools to create meaningful and impactful changes. These different categories of workshops include:

Gender-Sensitive School Policymaking

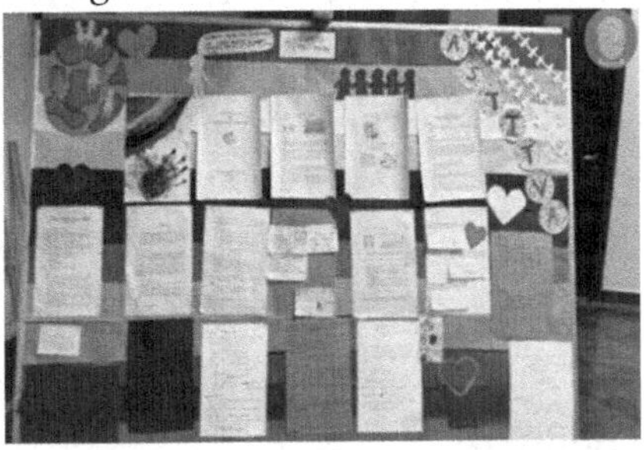

Objective: Students engaged with a guest expert from the policymaking sector to understand the intricacies of policy creation. They collaborated to develop frameworks and proposals that aimed to foster a gender-inclusive school environment and ensure institutional support for LGBTQIA+ students.

Media for Advocacy (Digital Media)

Objective: A marketing expert conducted a session on the power of media in social advocacy. Students learnt about digital storytelling, effective audience engagement, and how media platforms can be leveraged to advocate for LGBTQIA+ rights and representation.

Art as Expression (Fashion & Painting)

Objective: Under the guidance of a professional artist and fashion designer, students explored traditional and contemporary art forms to express themes of identity, diversity, and inclusion. This hands-on session encouraged creative exploration through various artistic media.

This event was structured to challenge existing norms and encourage proactive action. Chief guests and professionals from various fields were invited to engage with students, ensuring a comprehensive and immersive learning experience. The event featured a talk by the Chief Guest, and the founder shared her personal experiences.

An Identity Session was conducted by a Student Counselor, followed by engaging workshops and an exhibition showcasing the work created by the students. The event concluded with a closing ceremony. Altogether, the event educated students about community and allyship, and instilled skills to regulate emotions and become more empathetic and accepting towards others.

Fundraiser: Pause for a Cause

Astitva Teens has also organized multiple fundraisers to support its ongoing projects and initiatives. Its first fundraising event was a combined bake sale and book sale, held to ensure an orderly flow and prevent overcrowding. The entire process was a collaborative effort—students baked goods at home, carefully determined pricing, designed posters, and worked together to host the sale. While the event was a success, we encountered

challenges in crowd management, underscoring the need for improved coordination and timely communication. Despite these hurdles, the fundraiser demonstrated teamwork, communication, and a shared commitment to creating a more inclusive space. The proceeds from the bake sale were dedicated to funding future *Astitva Teens* projects and initiatives supporting the LGBTQIA+ community.

Building on the success of the first bake sale, a second one was organized at an exhibition showcasing student physics

projects. This was on a larger scale, with increased student participation and a significant presence of parents. To raise awareness, we distributed flyers about *Astitva Teens* and displayed posters outlining ways to be an ally to the LGBTQIA+ community. This fundraiser not only helped secure funds for our initiatives but also provided an opportunity to educate and engage a broader audience in meaningful conversations about inclusivity. These sales exemplify our belief that even small actions can contribute to larger societal change, reinforcing the importance of community support in fostering a more accepting environment.

Expanding Our Digital Presence and Educational Outreach

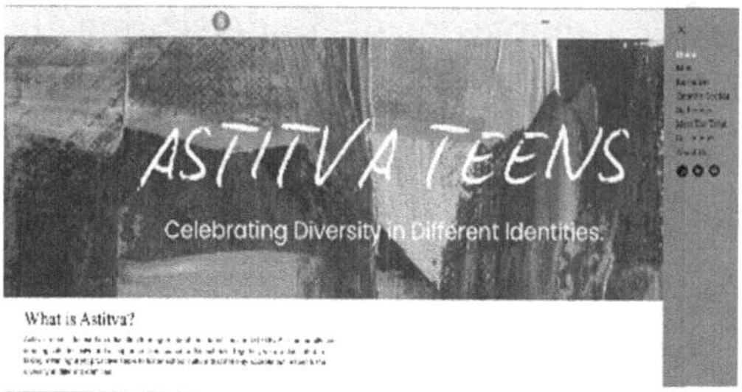

Recognizing the increasing influence of digital platforms in educating and engaging young audiences, *Astitva Teens* has launched its official website. The website serves as a repository of weekly blogs, educational resources, and creative submissions from students across various schools. It aims to provide insightful content on LGBTQIA+ topics, allyship, and inclusivity, allowing individuals to broaden their perspectives and deepen their understanding of the community.

Additionally, the creative section of the website offers a dedicated space for students to express themselves through poetry, art, photography, and media creations. This initiative ensures that student voices are both heard and celebrated, fostering an environment where artistic and personal expressions are encouraged. Submissions are reviewed and uploaded by the team, with external student contributions welcomed and encouraged. To further

enhance awareness, *Astitva Teens* has established a presence on multiple social media platforms, including YouTube, Instagram, and LinkedIn. These platforms cater to diverse audiences and serve as tools for advocacy, education, and outreach. The goal is to harness the power of digital media to effectively engage teenagers and create an inclusive online community.

Newsletter Initiative: Encouraging Inclusive Practices

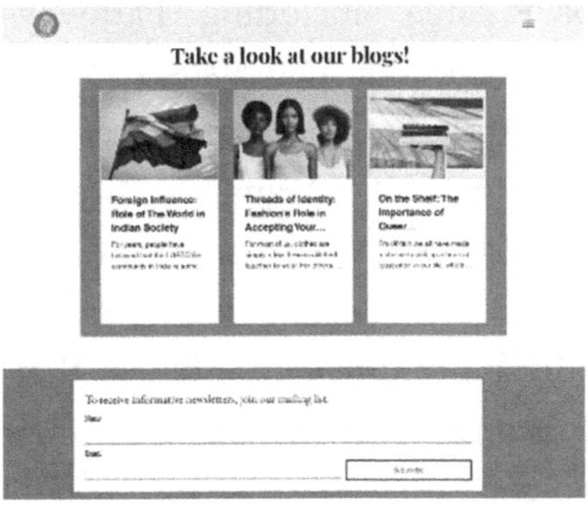

Astitva Teens has also launched a newsletter service open to all individuals interested in learning more about LGBTQIA+ issues and allyship. The newsletter features practical steps that individuals can take to become better allies, such as incorporating pronouns in email signatures. Additionally, it highlights key blog topics, shares useful resources, and keeps subscribers updated on upcoming initiatives and events. The newsletter aims to serve as a consistent source of knowledge and awareness, inspiring readers to actively support and advocate for the LGBTQIA+ community.

A Collaborative Team: Strength in Diversity

Astitva Teens operates with a dedicated team of 15-20 students from different grades, ranging from middle school to collegiate levels. This diverse team structure allows for mentorship opportunities, where younger students learn from their senior peers, fostering leadership development and collaborative learning. The team works collectively to conceptualize, plan, and execute various initiatives, ensuring a dynamic and inclusive approach to advocacy.

Expanding Our Impact: Partnerships with Other Schools

Beyond our home institution, *Astitva Teens* has extended its reach to other schools in the Delhi NCR area, including Pathways World School, Pathways Aravalli, DPS International, and The Shri Ram School, Aravalli. Through workshops, discussions, and policy advocacy, we aim to educate students, address their concerns, and ensure that their voices are heard by school authorities. By collaborating with multiple institutions, *Astitva Teens* is committed to creating systemic change in educational spaces and fostering environments where diversity is respected and celebrated.

Astitva Teens continues to be a driving force for LGBTQIA+ education, awareness, and action within schools and digital platforms. Through structured events, digital outreach, and collaborative partnerships, we are committed to shaping a future where inclusivity is not just discussed but actively implemented. Our mission remains clear—to empower teenagers with knowledge, amplify their voices, and create safe spaces that nurture identity, acceptance, and advocacy.

Future Aspiration of Astitva Teens

Filing a Public Interest Litigation (PIL) with the Ministry of Education

Astitva Teens is dedicated to driving systemic change through advocacy for the inclusion of LGBTQIA+ education in school curricula. As part of our forthcoming initiatives, we are planning to file a Public Interest Litigation (PIL) with the Ministry of Education, advocating for the integration of comprehensive information on gender identity, sexual orientation, and inclusivity into school textbooks. This effort aims to ensure that students are provided with accurate, age-appropriate information on these topics, thereby fostering awareness, empathy, and acceptance from an early age. By striving for policy-level changes, we aim to create a more inclusive academic environment where LGBTQIA+ students feel seen, supported, and safe. In collaboration with legal experts, activists, and educators, we will develop a robust case that highlights the need for a curriculum that reflects the diverse realities of all students.

Launching an App

Astitva Teens is in the process of developing an app, scheduled for launch in July 2025, which will provide a secure platform for youth to express themselves, connect with others facing similar challenges, and access critical support. Key features will include anonymous support groups, 24/7 paid counseling services, and resources to promote inclusive behavior and language use. The app will also offer dedicated support groups for both parents and children, acknowledging the difficulties families face during the coming-out process. Furthermore, the app will feature a mental health tracking tool, enabling users to log their emotions, with professionals monitoring for signs of distress or suicidal thoughts. Webinars and virtual meetups with experts will also be held, promoting education and fostering connection. Our aim is to create an inclusive and supportive space where every individual feels heard, accepted, and valued.

Voices

Self-love & Acceptance: The key to true confidence
By SONIA BEMBI SETH (Chief Life Designer)

Valentine's Day is a celebration of love, but what if I tell you that the most important love is the one you have for yourself? In a world filled with social media filters, grades, peer pressure, and constant comparisons, many teenagers seek validation from external sources—likes, comments, and approval from others. However, the truth is that no amount of external validation can ever fill the void of self-doubt unless you truly accept yourself from within.

Love Begins With You
Imagine looking into a mirror and saying, "I am enough." That is where self-acceptance starts. If someone criticizes you, it only affects you when, deep down, you believe it to be true. Think about this: if someone tells you that you have green hair, would it bother you? No! Because you know your hair is not green. But if someone calls you a failure, and you feel hurt, it is because somewhere inside, you fear that it might be true.
Here is the SECRET!

How we talk to ourselves validates how we respond to others, which ultimately shapes our experiences.
Legendary author Jack Canfield, in his best-selling book *Chicken Soup for the Soul,* introduced a simple yet powerful formula: **E + R = O** *(Event + Response = Outcome)*

You may not always have control over the events in your life, but you DO have control over how you respond. If someone makes a hurtful comment, you can either let it affect your self-worth, or you can choose to remind yourself, "Their words do not define me. I define me."

Life Methodology

Taking 100% Responsibility
Taking 100% responsibility for your life means eliminating blame and complaints. It is about standing in your power and owning your actions. When you take full responsibility, you regain control and step out of a victim mindset. The shift from "Why is this happening to me?" to "How can I grow from this?" is life-changing.

Work on Your Courage
Courage is not about fearlessness; it's about acting despite fear.

Ask yourself:

- What was the time when you truly showed courage?
- What did you learn from that experience?
- What would you pursue in life if fear did not hold you back? Imagine you could not fail—what dreams would you chase?

A Simple Ritual for Self-Love is Letting Go

Here is a fun and easy activity to remind yourself that love flows from within:

- Make a heart with your hands and say: *LET THEM BE.*
- Put your hand away from you and say: *LET IT GO.*
- Do a high-five gesture and say: *LET'S DO IT!*
- Make waves with your hands and say: *LET IT FLOW.*

Love is not about changing yourself for others; it is about embracing who you already are.

Heal the World, One Heart at a Time

Instead of judging others, let's accept that every person is doing the best they can with what they know. Their judgments are reflections of their own inner struggles. If we practice empathy, we can truly heal the world and make it a better place for everyone.

Look in the mirror and say: I am worthy. I am enough. I am loved. Let's make self-love the most celebrated love of all.

Part III

Educational Content of the Book

– Chapter 4 –
Blogs about the LGBTQIA+ Community and Allyship

Index

1. **From Hashtags to Movements: The Role of Social Media on LGBTQIA+ Awareness**

   Social media has transformed LGBTQIA+ awareness, offering visibility, support, and activism on a global scale. Platforms like Instagram, Facebook, and X enable queer individuals to share their stories, educate others, and build communities, breaking geographic barriers and reducing isolation. For LGBTQIA+ youth, social media provides access to role models, educational content, and safe spaces for self-exploration. The digital world has also amplified activism, fostering acceptance and allyship. As these platforms continue evolving, their role in advocating for queer rights and inclusion will only grow, shaping a more informed and accepting society.

2. **What Makes a Family: A Queer Perspective on Family Building**

   Family is more thavn biology—it is about love, support, and connection. For LGBTQIA+ individuals, building a family often means overcoming legal barriers and societal stigma, leading many to form chosen families based on acceptance and shared values. Parenthood within the queer community takes diverse forms, from adoption and surrogacy to co-parenting. Despite challenges like legal recognition and discrimination, queer families redefine traditional norms, proving that love, not convention, defines family. By embracing these evolving perspectives, society can create inclusive spaces where all families—whether biological or chosen—are recognized, celebrated, and supported in their journey toward love and a sense of belonging.

3. **Faith vs Identity: Finding a Common Ground**

The intersection of faith and LGBTQIA+ identity can be challenging, as many religious teachings have historically excluded queer individuals. This has led to internal conflicts and external rejection, forcing many to choose between faith and identity. However, resilience has led to reinterpretations of religious texts and the creation of inclusive faith communities. Scholars like Matthew Vines and Rabbi Steven Greenberg advocate for LGBTQIA+ inclusion within religious traditions. Organizations such as Q Christian Fellowship provide support. As faith communities evolve, the possibility of harmony between faith and identity grows, fostering spaces where both can be embraced and celebrated.

4. **The Queer Experience in Rural vs Urban Areas**

Queer experiences vary greatly between rural and urban areas, shaping access to support, visibility, and safety. Cities often provide larger, more accepting LGBTQIA+ communities, pride events, and legal protections, while rural areas can be isolating with fewer resources and stronger traditional norms. Discrimination may be lower in urban settings, yet challenges persist. In contrast, rural queer individuals may face greater risks of harassment and social exclusion. Despite these disparities, advocacy and education can bridge the gap, fostering inclusivity in all spaces. Ensuring resources and acceptance reach every corner is key to supporting queer individuals everywhere.

5. **From Algorithms to Allyship: How is AI Supporting the Community?**

   AI is playing a growing role in supporting the LGBTQIA+ community by fostering allyship, inclusion, and mental well-being. AI-driven chatbots and therapy apps provide crucial mental health support, particularly for those without access to traditional therapy. AI also enhances online safety by detecting and reducing discriminatory content while amplifying LGBTQIA+ voices. In education, AI-powered learning tools help spread awareness and affirm queer identities. As AI continues to evolve, it has the potential to break barriers and create safer, more inclusive spaces. Ethical implementation remains key to ensuring AI remains a tool for empowerment, advocacy, and equality.

6. **LGBTQIA+ Youth Homelessness and Its Impacts**

   LGBTQIA+ youth homelessness is a growing issue driven by family rejection, discrimination, and aging out of foster care. Without stable housing, queer youth face deteriorating mental health, barriers to education and employment, and increased safety risks. Discrimination in housing and shelters further limits their options, making survival even harder. Solutions like LGBTQIA+-inclusive housing programs and protective legislation can provide stability and security, helping these individuals rebuild their lives. Addressing this crisis is crucial to ensuring that all youth have safe and supportive environments where they can thrive and work toward a brighter future.

7. **Diversity in the Lab: LGBTQIA+ Voices in STEM**
   LGBTQIA+ representation in STEM is vital for fostering diversity, innovation, and inclusivity. Despite historical marginalization, many queer scientists have made groundbreaking contributions while paving the way for future generations. Representation brings fresh perspectives, enhances problem-solving, and inspires young LGBTQIA+ individuals to pursue STEM careers without fear. Figures like Tim Cook and Sally Ride demonstrate that queer individuals have made significant contributions to STEM fields. By promoting inclusivity through supportive policies and visibility, we can ensure that all identities are valued in the lab, leading to a more equitable and forward-thinking scientific community.

8. **Healing the Gap in Trans Healthcare**
   Transgender individuals face significant barriers in healthcare due to stigma, a lack of trained professionals, and limited access, especially in rural areas. These challenges lead to physical health issues like inadequate hormone regulation and mental health struggles such as depression and anxiety. Addressing this gap requires comprehensive training for medical professionals, inclusive healthcare policies, and accessible mental health

support. Ensuring trans individuals receive respectful and knowledgeable care is essential for their well-being. By implementing systemic changes and fostering inclusivity, we can bridge the gap in trans healthcare and ensure equitable medical access for all, regardless of gender identity.

9. **From Shame to Pride: Reclaiming Your Identity**
   Reclaiming identity from shame to pride is a powerful journey for LGBTQIA+ individuals, challenging societal norms and internalized stigma. Rooted in religious beliefs, cultural expectations, and bullying, queer shame leads to self-doubt and fear. Overcoming it involves self-acceptance, finding affirming communities, seeking representation, engaging in activism, and accessing therapy. Pride extends beyond celebrations, manifesting in everyday authenticity and community support. By embracing pride, individuals resist marginalization and inspire future generations. Though the journey is not linear, fostering self-worth and visibility creates a more inclusive world where every queer person can look in the mirror with pride, not shame.

10. **Hidden Wounds: Bullying in Indian Schools**
    Bullying in Indian schools remains a critical issue, particularly for students who do not conform to societal norms. Despite uniforms meant to promote equality, many face exclusion and discrimination, often worsened by educators themselves. Stories like Rohan's, where bullying led to isolation and fear, highlight the deep impact on students' mental well-being. A 2018 survey by the Centre

for Civil Society found that over 40% of students experienced bullying due to perceived differences. To create a truly inclusive learning space, schools must foster empathy and acceptance, ensuring that no student feels alone in their struggle for belonging.

11. **Bridging Identities: Intersectionality in the LGBTQ+ Community**

    Intersectionality in the LGBTQ+ community highlights how overlapping marginalized identities, such as race, disability, and socio-economic status, amplify discrimination. Cultural biases, accessibility barriers, and economic struggles make life more challenging for queer individuals from diverse backgrounds. For example, acceptance rates vary globally, and disabled LGBTQ+ individuals face exclusion from Pride events. Socio-economic disparities further limit job opportunities and housing security. To support intersectional identities, we must educate ourselves, advocate for inclusive policies, and amplify diverse voices. Embracing and understanding these layers of identity can help dismantle systemic power imbalances and create a more inclusive world.

12. **Beyond Labels: Gender-Neutral Washrooms for All**

    Gender-neutral washrooms in schools offer a safe and inclusive space for students of all gender identities, yet they remain a source of controversy. Many LGBTQIA+ students, especially transgender and non-binary youth, face daily anxiety and harassment when using gendered restrooms. Studies show high rates of bullying due to the lack of inclusive facilities. While solutions exist, such as converting single-stall restrooms or designating multi-stall gender-neutral spaces, resistance persists. The NCPCR opposed NCERT's proposal for such washrooms, citing psychological concerns, yet this stance reinforces exclusion. Schools must evolve to reflect the diversity of their societies, ensuring that all students feel safe, respected, and valued in their learning environments.

13. Queer Representation in Media

Queer representation in media is crucial for visibility, normalization, and acceptance. Research indicates that increased representation of LGBTQIA+ individuals positively impacts societal perceptions. However, representation must be diverse, moving beyond stereotypes of white, wealthy, gay men to include different races, ethnicities, abilities, and gender identities. Media portrayal varies—some franchises lack representation, while others misrepresent queer identities through harmful stereotypes. Positive representation, where queer characters are fully developed beyond their identities, fosters understanding. While achieving perfect representation takes time, advocating for inclusive and realistic portrayals ensures that the LGBTQIA+ community is seen, heard, and valued across all media platforms.

14. The Forgotten Connect Between Mythology and LGBTQ+

This piece beautifully dismantles the myth that LGBTQ+ identities are a Western import, grounding them in India's rich historical and mythological narratives. From the

Kama Sutra to the Ramayana and Mahabharata, ancient Indian texts openly acknowledged and even celebrated gender fluidity and same-sex relationships. The introduction of Section 377 by the British in 1860 marked a stark departure from this openness, shaping the conservative attitudes we see today. By revisiting these stories and embracing our true cultural history, we can bridge the gap between tradition and modernity, reaffirming that love, in all its forms, has always been part of India's legacy.

15. Discovering Self: How Online Communities Shape LGBTQIA+ Youth in India amid the Digital Chaos

This article highlights the profound impact of online communities on LGBTQIA+ youth in India, offering both a sanctuary for self-discovery and a potential battleground for harassment. While platforms like Tumblr, Instagram, and LGBTQIA+ Facebook groups provide validation and belonging, the **lack of offline support**—from families, schools, and media—makes the internet an essential but fragile refuge. The duality of empowerment and exposure underscores the urgent need for digital literacy programs, stronger cyberbullying laws, and more affirming virtual spaces, such as those created by Queerala and the Nazariya Foundation. To truly support LGBTQIA+ youth, **India must acknowledge, protect, and nurture these digital sanctuaries**, ensuring that the internet remains a bridge to self-acceptance rather than a site of fear.

16. **On the Shelf: The Importance of Queer Representation in Literature**

    Books shape our perceptions, whether we are avid readers or occasional ones. For LGBTQIA+ individuals, representation in literature fosters validation and normalizes identities, while for others, it expands understanding and empathy. Queer literature creates safe spaces and challenges stereotypes, making diverse and accurate portrayals essential. While authors like Adam Silvera and Becky Albertalli have made strides, gaps remain—more genres, intersectional identities, and varied narratives beyond romance are needed. True representation is not a trend but a necessity. By reading and promoting inclusive books, we contribute to a world where everyone's story is acknowledged, respected, and celebrated.

17. **Threads of Identity: Fashion's Role in Accepting Your Identity**

    Fashion is more than just fabric—it is a powerful tool for self-expression, especially in the LGBTQIA+ community. While society imposes rigid gender norms on clothing, queer fashion challenges these boundaries, enabling individuals to authentically express their identities. From Pride parades to everyday outfits, fashion communicates identity, fosters self-acceptance, and challenges stereotypes. By defying conventional expectations, queer individuals reclaim their right to wear what feels true to them. Ultimately, fashion is not just about trends but about visibility, individuality, and the freedom to express oneself without limitations. It is a statement: "I am who I am, and I wear it proudly."

18. **Foreign Influence: Role of the World in Indian Society**
    This piece humorously yet powerfully debunks the myth that LGBTQIA+ identities in India are a "Western influence," highlighting historical acceptance before colonial-era laws like Section 377 suppressed them. While the Supreme Court's 2018 decision decriminalized same-sex relationships, challenges remain—marriage equality is still out of reach. Corporate India is making strides with inclusive policies, but societal change is progressing at a slow pace. The real battle now is shifting mindsets—normalizing LGBTQIA+ identities in everyday life. From Pride celebrations to school safe spaces, young people play a key role in fostering acceptance. The fight is not just legal; it is about ensuring a future where everyone belongs.

19. **Calling Out vs. Calling In: What to do?**
    This chapter examines the distinction between calling out and calling in—two approaches to addressing harmful language or behaviour. Calling out is a public response that holds individuals accountable when immediate action is needed, while calling in involves private conversations to educate and encourage reflection. Understanding when to use each method is crucial in fostering change without unnecessary conflict. The chapter provides practical guidelines for both approaches, including conversation starters and strategies for navigating difficult discussions. By staying calm, using "I" statements, and focusing on

reflection, allies can effectively address harm and create a more inclusive and understanding environment.

20. **Coming Out and Self-Acceptance: Personal Journeys and Navigating Societal Pressures**
This chapter explores the challenges of coming out, emphasizing the safety concerns, societal pressures, and emotional impact it can have on LGBTQIA+ individuals. It highlights the importance of supportive environments in reducing mental health struggles and the role of cultural and religious perspectives in shaping acceptance. The chapter also addresses discrimination in the workplace and within organizations, while emphasizing the importance of self-acceptance. It reassures individuals that there is no right time or way to come out, encouraging them to move at their own pace. By finding role models, supportive communities, and trusted confidants, individuals can navigate their journey with confidence.

21. **Family and Acceptance**
This chapter examines the pivotal role of family in shaping the well-being and identity of LGBTQIA+ individuals. It highlights how familial acceptance can significantly impact mental health, reducing risks like depression and suicidal thoughts, while rejection can lead to severe emotional distress. Families may struggle with societal expectations, generational gaps, or fear of judgment, but understanding and education can foster acceptance. Research from the Family Acceptance Project suggests that supportive actions, such as affirming identities, defending against discrimination, and welcoming LGBTQIA+ peers,

can be beneficial. While families may not be perfect, learning and showing empathy can create a safer, more inclusive environment for their loved ones.

22. **Self-Acceptance and Empathy**
This chapter examines the relationship between self-acceptance and empathy within the LGBTQIA+ experience. Self-acceptance involves overcoming societal pressures, rejecting unrealistic expectations, and embracing one's identity. It is a journey, not a one-time achievement. Empathy plays a crucial role, as surrounding oneself with supportive people and shared experiences fosters a sense of self-worth. Practising empathy toward others can also strengthen self-acceptance. Strategies such as positive self-talk, affirmations, and building a strong support system can be helpful. Ultimately, recognizing one's value and embracing individuality leads to a fulfilling and confident life, reminding everyone that they are worthy of love and acceptance.

23. **Understanding Identities: Breaking down Gender, Sex, and Sexualities**
This chapter clarifies the differences between gender, sex, and sexuality, which are often confused or used interchangeably. Gender is a social construct related to identity, separate from the sex assigned at birth. Sex refers to biological traits but does not dictate gender identity. Sexuality is an individual's personal identity, encompassing gender, sex, and attraction. Identities can be fluid and do not need to conform to societal labels. Understanding these distinctions fosters greater awareness

and inclusivity, ensuring that everyone's identity is acknowledged and respected. Ultimately, identity is personal, evolving, and uniquely yours.

24. What to Do If a Friend Comes Out to You?

This chapter provides guidance on how to respond when a friend comes out to you, emphasizing the importance of listening, affirming their identity, and respecting their pace. It outlines supportive actions, such as using correct pronouns and asking what they need, while also cautioning against harmful behaviors like invalidating their experience or outing them. True allyship goes beyond the moment, requiring ongoing education, advocacy, and regular check-ins. By fostering a supportive environment, you can help your friend feel safe, valued, and accepted for who they are.

25. Understanding Pronouns and Language Why Inclusive Language Matters

This chapter examines the importance of pronouns and inclusive language in promoting respect and affirmation for individuals' identities. It highlights why using correct pronouns matters, how to introduce them in conversations, and the impact of misgendering on mental health. The chapter also provides practical tips for getting pronouns right, normalizing their use, and avoiding assumptions based on appearance or assigned sex. By adopting inclusive language, individuals and organizations can create safer and more supportive environments for everyone, ensuring that all identities are acknowledged and respected.

– From Hashtags to Movements –

The Role of Social Media on LGBTQIA+ Awareness

Whether it is a global issue or the latest film, we usually receive our daily updates with the help of social media. From its early days as a simple communication tool, it has evolved into a massive platform where people share information, build communities, and raise awareness. Today, it serves as a dynamic space that enables not only self-expression but also opens doors to activism, education, and global awareness. For the queer community, Social Media is a method to find support, visibility, and confidence in ways that were previously difficult. In other words, it has revolutionized LGBTQIA+ awareness.

Amplifying Visibility

With millions of users on platforms such as Instagram, Facebook, and X, social media posts have one of the largest audiences available, enabling queer individuals to share their stories openly. Posts can be viewed, liked, and shared, which helps extend the audience to include the people who receive the message. LGBTQIA+ individuals share stories, experiences, and some even educate online, thus helping break down stereotypes and normalize the presence of queer people in life. Additionally, by seeing others express themselves, people can feel less alone and more motivated, and allies gain insights into the queer experience.

Creating Communities

From group conversations on Instagram, which can include up to 250 individual accounts, to Facebook Communities, Social Media has a platform for everyone to form empowering communities. Today, you can easily search for communities that interest you and join them, which gives queer people the chance to connect with others who have similar experiences. Not only does this allow for the exchange of advice, but these communities also provide emotional support and a safe space to explore one's identity.

Breaking Geographic Limits

For LGBTQIA+ individuals in less accepting or more isolated communities, Social Media is a bridge to create and connect with a community. Not only does this allow people to accept themselves, but it also reduces isolation and empowers individuals to live authentically, regardless of their location.

Impact on Youth

With the changing generations, social media has had a greater impact on our lives than ever before, particularly for young people. LGBTQIA+ youth can anonymously explore identity, find educational material, find role models, and see diverse experiences. This helps reduce stigma amongst audiences and can be especially great for those who do not have access to supportive environments.

In the end, social media has undoubtedly transformed the landscape for queer awareness, visibility, and activism. It has broken isolation, amplified stories, and created a platform for support. As these platforms continue to evolve, their power to educate, empower, and spread awareness within the

LGBTQIA+ community will only grow, further promoting acceptance.

How Legal Protection Shapes Queer Lives

Legal Protection - more than just words on paper, they are lifelines to many people for upholding dignity, equality, and our fundamental rights. For the LGBTQIA+ community, the presence (or absence) of legal protections and laws has a significant effect on daily life, whether it is safety or finding a job. Let's explore how vital legal frameworks are in maintaining the standard of living for queer individuals.

Safety and Security

Discrimination, hate crimes, and violence are some of the many challenges queer individuals face, and protection from the same is crucial for a person's safety and security. If not provided, the lack of legal protection can lead to bad experiences in workplaces, schools, and public spaces, especially for trans and non-binary individuals. By holding people accountable with the help of laws, we can create safer surroundings. For example, the Matthew Shepard and James Byrd Jr. Hate Crimes Prevention Act, enacted by the USA in 2009, ensured that protection from hate crime extends to LGBTQIA+ individuals. This statute gave LGBTQIA+ communities a crucial safety net by strengthening the capacity to prosecute crimes driven by sexual orientation or gender identity.

In addition, a legal framework can provide security amongst families, especially by legalizing same-sex marriage. From inheritance rights to child custody, it ensures that all families are protected under the law. For example, the

Obergefell v. Hodges decision in the USA legitimized same-sex marriage and created security for couples.

Supporting Mental Health

Legal affirmations can also convey a powerful message of inclusion, thereby improving the self-esteem and acceptance of queer individuals. Because of prejudice and stigma in society, queer people frequently experience higher levels of stress and legal protection not only gives peace of mind, but can help reduce these negative activities. For example, in Argentina, the 2012 Gender Identity Law empowers transgender individuals to have their personal documents registered with their proper name and gender and to be treated in keeping with their gender identity.

Economic Equality

Another common barrier the queer community faces falls into economic categories, more specifically, the discrimination in employment and housing. Legal protection that prohibits bias can ensure that LGBTQIA+ individuals have equal opportunities to earn a livelihood and live in a safe environment.

In conclusion, ensuring safety, fostering equality, and affirming all identities can be done with the help of legal protections. These can significantly shape lives by reducing discrimination, supporting mental health, and kindling opportunities for financial and economic stability. While progress has been made in our world today, continued efforts can guarantee a more inclusive world.

– What Makes a Family –

A Queer Perspective on Family Building

The cornerstone of human connection, our families have shaped us to be the people we are today. From providing love and support to being key players in forming our personality, the people we grow up with are the stepping stones to our success. However, the traditional concept of a family can sometimes overshadow what it truly means to be one. The typical picture of a nuclear, heteronormative, and biologically related family is far from universal. The concept of a family extends beyond social conventions and should be founded on love, mutual respect, and strong bonds. For LGBTQIA+ individuals, creating a family and kindling this bond can be a little more difficult. From legal restrictions to societal expectations and stigma, queer people are always faced with challenges in this department. This can not only stop them from finding love, but it can also lead to severe mental issues and be detrimental to their wellness. Rather, in today's ever-evolving world, we must look at families from a fresh perspective that breaks the barrier of social conventions, thus giving everyone, including queer individuals, the opportunity to build a family.

The Role of Chosen Family

Emotional support, gaining life experience, and finding a safe space are some of the reasons families are our lifelines, but this does not have to be limited to biological families. Estrangement from biological families due to an unaccepting nature or rejection can lead to LGBTQIA+ people feeling alone, and a chosen family can help change that. They are built on mutual care, shared values, and unconditional acceptance—qualities that often transcend biology. Chosen families affirm the idea that love, rather than blood, is the binding force of human connection, because sometimes "The blood of the covenant is thicker than the water of the womb".

Diverse Paths to Parenthood

Within the queer community, parenthood is varied and diverse as the community itself. Through various routes, the community is redefining parenthood.

- **Adoption and Fostering:** This is a common route, and many queer individuals pick this as a path to parenthood. Not only does this bring up the opportunity to nurture a child, but it also aligns with the values of inclusivity. Despite some legal challenges, most LGBTQIA+ parents' joy outweighs the struggles they face.
- **Surrogacy or Assisted Reproduction:** Technological advancements have opened new avenues for same-sex couples to have children, either with surrogacy, sperm donors, etc. While it may be costly and present legal challenges, it provides the opportunity to have a biological connection with children.
- **Co-Parenting:** Some queer people may also choose to co-parent with family or friends. This is primarily rooted in shared responsibility along with clear and concise communication, which showcases a commitment to creating a loving environment.

Overcoming Challenges

While many queer parents have been able to experience the sheer and utter joy of building a family, whether biological or chosen, some people may face some challenges along the way. Legal recognition still remains a hurdle in many places; for example, same-sex marriage is not legally recognized in India. Social stigma and discrimination further complicate matters, requiring advocacy and education to reduce biases.

In conclusion, the new perspectives on family building brought about by queer individuals challenge traditional norms and help celebrate diverse and unique families. By valuing and embracing these new paths, we can find a safe and loving home for every person.

– Faith vs Identity –

Finding a Common Ground

The intersection of faith and identity can be both a source of strength and a site of conflict, particularly for LGBTQ+ individuals. For many, they turn to their faith to find purpose, meaning and moral guidance. Yet, many religious institutions and teachings do not support the queer community, leading to both internal and external struggles for them. Despite this, many queer individuals long for respect, if not support, and are finding paths to reconcile their faith and identity, to calm the turmoil of their clash.

Historically, some religious institutions have excluded LGBTQIA+ individuals, saying that their identities are incompatible with the religions. This has made queer individuals who seek to find peace in religion feel alienated.

This divide has often created a black-and-white situation, where many have been asked to choose. Reor Faith? This conflict is deeply personal, and the desire to live authentically and connect with their faith can lead to feelings of anxiety and confusion.

Even while facing these challenges, the religious queer community has showcased resilience by finding solace in their own ways, whether through reinterpretation or the creation of inclusive spaces. This resilience underscores a profound truth: faith and identity are not at odds but can help guide a person together. Many scholars have also revisited texts to affirm identities. This includes the likes of:

- Matthew Vines: Aims to advance LGBTQIA+ inclusion in the church.
- Pamela R. Lightsey: Advocates for Black & Queer Theology.
- Rabbi Steven Greenberg: Argues for reinterpretations that recognize queer dignity, along with remaining faithful to Jewish tradition.

In the end, we must look towards building inclusive communities like many faith communities worldwide are evolving to include and celebrate LGBTQIA+ individuals. The United Church of Christ, the Metropolitan Community Church, and Reform Judaism have taken steps to affirm queer members through the implementation of inclusive policies. It showcases how we can evolve to maintain dignity. In addition, organizations like The Trevor Project and Q Christian Fellowship also help navigate the intersection between faith and identity, thus working towards fostering a sense of belonging.

Faith and identity, although often perceived as conflicting, can coexist and even complement each other. Overcoming challenges will, of course, be a part of the journey, but the resilience we showcase is a testament to the common human spirit we share. By embracing people of all kinds and welcoming them into our communities, we can create spaces where faith and identity are both celebrated.

– The Queer Experience in Rural vs Urban Areas –

Our world spans from cities to villages, from mountains to beaches, and wherever we are, there are always a diverse set of people we can meet. But sometimes, the experiences unique individuals face, such as those in the LGBTQIA+ community, can differ based on geographic location. Different places can offer vastly differing challenges and opportunities, which require distinctive solutions and adaptations to live comfortably, from access to support to finding communities—the place where a queer individual lives can shape how they navigate their life.

Visibility and Community Support

In urban areas, there are usually larger communities, which are more diverse, making it easier for queer individuals to find supportive and healthy LGBTQIA+ communities. Many cities also tend to host pride parades, Queer Events, have dedicated safe spaces, and have a more positive mindset towards the group. This visibility can make it easier for individuals to connect with others who share similar experiences.

In contrast, these resources are sometimes scarce in rural places, making queer people feel alone. Rural citizens may find it difficult to get community support due to the lower representation and lower number of openly LGBTQIA+ people, which can result in feelings of invisibility or loneliness. Sometimes, low internet access may limit access to online communities that are also available.

Discrimination

It is common knowledge that urban regions are more progressive and have better safeguards against violence and prejudice. These areas are not immune to discrimination. Although the levels of discrimination are significantly lower, some urban areas might still be dangerous for LGBTQIA+ people.

On the other hand, coming out or being your authentic self may be a little more dangerous in rural areas, especially due to the extremely traditional and conservative norms followed there. To add on, LGBTQIA+ people may be more vulnerable in some rural areas due to a lack of legal safeguards and a higher prevalence of harassment and discrimination.

For example, a trans individual in a rural town, which has limited communication with the modern world and adheres to extremely traditional practices, may face hostility in many areas; meanwhile, a city individual will have access to affirming institutions.

Social Dynamics

In urban areas, the larger and more diverse population is generally more accepting and has a more inclusive mindset. People who identify themselves as queer can feel more comfortable expressing themselves without worrying about being rejected by their families or social networks.

Meanwhile, traditional values prevail in close-knit rural communities, and there may be a lot of pressure to fit in. Some queer people may choose to hide their identities out of fear of rejection or disapproval.

The distinct queer experiences in rural and urban areas underscore the significance of community and environment in the lives of queer individuals. While cities offer more resources, visibility, support, and acceptance, rural areas lack some of these qualities. By covering up these gaps with the help of advocacy and education, we can ensure queer individuals thrive everywhere.

– From Algorithms to Allyship –

How Is AI supporting the Community?

Artificial Intelligence, more commonly known as AI, is rapidly growing and transforming various sectors, including medicine and entertainment. However, even with its massive success in highly technical areas, there is one situation where its significance is growing day by day: its ability to support marginalized communities, including the queer community. By promoting understanding and acceptance, AI has the potential to create safer spaces and amplify the voices of LGBTQIA+ individuals. As an advocate for visibility, inclusion, and allyship, AI is supporting the community and will continue to do so. Here's how:

Support for Mental Health and Well-Being

Discrimination, isolation, and stigma are the issues faced by members of the LGBTQIA+ community, and some people are left to face them without a support system or a person to talk to. But AI is changing that. Chatbots, Therapy Apps, and Online Platforms are being created with the help of AI to provide support in a safe, convenient, and anonymous way. Platforms like Wysa and Woebot offer therapies, stress management methods, and mindfulness exercises, all of which can help queer individuals with their mental state. This is particularly helpful for those who live in areas where traditional therapy may not be available, thus showcasing how AI is also breaking down geographical barriers and providing immediate support, which can be vital for those in need of assistance.

AI-Powered Allyship AI can be a useful tool in online monitoring and safety to protect communities. It is doing so by identifying and addressing discriminatory content online. By training Artificial Intelligence to detect harmful content and flag discriminatory posts, online harassment can be reduced. In addition, AI can help amplify the voices of LGBTQIA+ activists and community leaders. For example, it can target specific audiences who are more likely to share allyship content, thereby spreading the message further and reaching new people. In other words, AI can enable effective identification of threats and mitigate them and can support campaigns advocating for equality, justice, and legislative improvements.

Inclusive Education and Learning Tools

AI-powered education platforms can help spread awareness and knowledge about the LGBTQIA+ community amongst others. Adaptive learning technologies can affirm queer identities and provide safe and supportive materials. For those who do not know much about the community, AI-based education can be used to create educational content for awareness and advocacy.

In the end, AI is an invaluable ally for the LGBTQIA+ community. As AI technology continues to evolve, its ability to break down barriers will also increase, enabling it to reach a broader audience. However, it is imperative to maintain ethical guidelines that prioritize the well-being and safety of all individuals. By leveraging the power of AI, we can see a shift toward a more equitable and inclusive future for LGBTQIA+ individuals.

– LGBTQIA+ Youth Homelessness and Its Impacts–

A common problem many LGBTQIA+ youth face is homelessness. Whether due to an unaccepting community or financial strain, this problem continues to grow and is especially prominent in places like the USA. Family rejection, discrimination, and violence often force these young individuals out of their homes and onto the streets, leaving them vulnerable to a range of physical, emotional, and psychological challenges. With limited access to resources and education, the consequences can be devastating. This issue not only highlights the need for intervention but also the importance of a safe home for queer youth.

Causes of LGBTQIA+ Youth Homelessness

- Family Rejection — Many young people are rejected by their families due to their identity, and the pre-existing notions and beliefs of their families. This leads to adolescents and youngsters, who have not had the chance to experience the world, being left on the streets to fend for themselves.
- Discrimination — Discrimination by either real estate agents, brokers, landlords, or communities can limit the housing LGBTQIA+ young adults can find that fit their budget and needs. This can lead to either living in a house in an unsafe area or residing in a homeless shelter, which may also discriminate, thus depleting an individual's options.
- Aging Out of Foster Care — Queer youth who age out of foster care have both a lack of experience and support, and may face discriminatory behavior. This combination makes it even more challenging to find stable housing, another contributing factor to homelessness.

Impacts on LGBTQIA+ Youth

- Deteriorating Mental Health — One of the most prominent impacts of homelessness is deteriorating mental health amongst youth. Increased exposure to trauma and a lack of derogatory interactions, especially with family, leads to reduced self-esteem and confidence, and increases anxiety and paranoia, which is extremely bad for anyone's mental health.
- Education & Employment — Along with discrimination, having unstable housing or being

homeless can impact queer youth education and employment, which in turn leads to no source of stable income. Unstable housing, frequent moving, and concerns about one's safety make it more challenging to focus on schoolwork and attend the same school daily. Additionally, improper address documentation can hinder one's chances of getting a job or a stable source of income necessary to maintain housing.

- Safety Risks — While living on the street, LGBTQIA+ youth, especially those on the younger side, are further susceptible to exploitation, including human trafficking. This is also bad for mental health.

Solutions and Interventions

- Housing Programs — The introduction of stable and legal housing programs for LGBTQIA+ youth can significantly enhance their mental and physical well-being. By being in a safe environment with proper access to basic human needs, youth can plan their life and connect with people in similar situations, thus improving their mental health. In addition, transitional housing, which slowly increases individual responsibility and introduces small amounts of rent, can help build stability and independence.
- Legislation — Policy and legislation are crucial for protection and fairness for queer youth. Housing protection, public accommodations, workplace protection, and other measures can all help homeless queer individuals get back on track.

In a nutshell, family rejection and discrimination are key causes of LGBTQIA+ youth homelessness, which puts their safety and mental health in danger. Implementing preventive measures and providing stable housing helps these young people start anew and secure a better future. To build an inclusive and supportive community, this issue must be addressed.

– Diversity in the Lab –

LGBTQIA+ Voices in STEM

Science, technology, engineering, and mathematics (STEM) have long been at the center of discovery and innovation, but these fields have in the past been largely dominated by those who seem to fit the traditional mold. For a long time, LGBTQIA+ individuals have faced marginalization in the field, with societal perspectives, often limiting what they could have contributed in the field. From scientists like Alan Turing, who hid their true identity, to many others who were unable to express themselves or were shunned for doing so, STEM has not always been inclusive of diverse identities.

Despite these challenges, many LGBTQIA+ scientists have made significant contributions to science, paving the way for future generations to be more accepting in the field. Their experiences underscore the importance of diversity in the lab, promoting equality, visibility, and acceptance, while also fostering creativity and innovation.

The Importance of LGBTQIA+ Representation in STEM

Different and diverse people always bring unique perspectives and ways of thinking, thus showcasing the need to include unique individuals in the field of STEM. Especially in fields like healthcare, where empathy towards everyone's experiences is crucial, the inclusion of queer individuals who understand others like themselves can revolutionize the effectiveness of services like medicine. Not only that, but the challenges queer individuals face give them a knack for critical thinking and problem-solving, crucial qualities in scientists. Additionally, increased visibility can inspire the next generation of LGBTQIA+ individuals to pursue their passions in STEM, rather than being obscured by fear. Knowing that they can succeed in this field without hiding their identity is a game-changer for the youth's mindsets and well-being.

Notable LGBTQIA+ Figures in STEM

With that, let us appreciate and acknowledge the powerful forces in STEM who happen to be part of the LGBTQIA+ community and have made significant contributions to the field of STEM.

- Tim Cook – More commonly known as the CEO of the worldwide technology brand Apple, Tim Cook is a prominent gay figure in technology. With his leadership, Apple has reached new heights and helped change the culture at the Company, inspiring other queer individuals in STEM.
- Sally Ride – A physicist, astronaut, and the first American woman to travel to space, Sally Ride has made many significant contributions to her field. Although it was not revealed during her lifetime, she was in a long-term relationship with another woman. Her legacy continues to inspire youth to explore space and express themselves.

In conclusion, LGBTQIA+ scientists have made numerous contributions despite the challenges they faced. Rest assured that upcoming generations of queer people are equipped to produce their own ground-breaking discoveries. By promoting supportive policies, creating inclusive spaces, and increasing LGBTQIA+ visibility, we can achieve this. The legacies of individuals like Tim Cook and Sally Ride serve as a reminder that diversity is crucial to scientific advancement and that STEM fields can be enhanced when all people, regardless of their identity, can be authentic in the lab.

– Healing the Gap in Trans Healthcare –

As our world continues to grow, advance, and develop in various fields, we have witnessed significant advancements in the field of medicine. However, sometimes it cannot cater to everyone. Transgender individuals often face barriers when trying to receive healthcare due to a multitude of reasons, which can be harmful for their physical and mental health. It is a complex issue rooted in stigma due to a lack of education and awareness. Therefore, addressing this gap is crucial to ensure that everyone can receive the healthcare they deserve, alongside being respected.

Causes of the Gap

- Stigma – Discrimination and Stigma amongst the community, healthcare workers, and healthcare administrators can lead to an individual either being denied care or being too afraid to ask for it. Prejudice and mistreatment also contribute to mistrust and avoidance, something which is not desired in a healthy relationship between a medical provider and patient, who must be treated with respect.

- Lack of Trained Individuals – Many doctors, nurses, physicians, etc., do not have the knowledge or training to treat transgender patients, especially in more suburban or rural areas. This not only stresses out the patient, but it can also have drastic impacts in the event of incorrect administration of medicine or medical procedures.
- Limited Access – In some areas, especially rural ones, treatment for transgender individuals is scarce and usually non-existent, making finding proper care even more difficult.

Impacts

- Physical Health – Without access to proper medical care, transgender people may face many negative outcomes, especially those related to hormones. Some include inadequate hormone regulation, which can lead to a loss of bone density.
- Mental Health – Since our health is usually interconnected, the physical health issues caused by the lack of access to medical healthcare can translate to mental health issues. This includes depression, anxiety, and low self-confidence.

Solutions

- Training and Education – Providing access to proper training in the field of trans health is crucial for ensuring that medical professionals can administer care and have a stronger level of trust with their transgender patients.

- Healthcare Policies — Inclusive healthcare policies which ensure that trans individuals are respected and not denied care are essential to alleviate financial burdens and ensure that transgender individuals have access to necessary care.
- Mental Health Support — Improving general well-being can be achieved with comprehensive mental health care that affirms transgender identities and addresses the particular difficulties they encounter.

In the end, healthcare is a basic human right which should be accessible to all. By systematic changes, we can begin to heal the gap in trans healthcare to ensure that they can live fulfilling, healthy lives, regardless of their gender.

– From Shame to Pride: Reclaiming your Identity –

The LGBTQIA+ community has often struggled with societal, cultural, and internalized shame around their unique identities. From hiding their true self to not accepting themselves, this stigma is harmful to mental health and well-being. Usually a result of discrimination, stigmatization, and rejection, continued shame should be something we strive to eliminate. The journey from hiding yourself to being proud in the open is a powerful narrative of resilience and self-discovery, as you identify your own self-worth. It is not just a personal victory but a transformative act that helps challenge societal norms.

The Roots of Queer Shame

Queer shame is deeply rooted in the mindset that being heterosexual is the default option. It is further reinforced by:

- **Religion:** Many religions do not accept queer identities, which can also disconnect a person from their faith and core beliefs.
- **Cultural Expectations:** Societies often expect people to conform to traditional gender roles and find the diversity of the LGBTQIA+ community "weird" and "unnatural", thus leading to shame within members.
- **Bullying and Rejection:** Typically originating from schoolyard taunts or workplace discrimination, hostility can lead to people being ashamed and even scared of who they truly are.

Internalizing these messages, which are already deeply ingrained in our society's mindsets, leads to self-doubt and low self-esteem. The shame is amplified by the fear of coming out and risking relationships, safety, and career opportunities.

The Path to Overcoming Shame

The transition from shame to pride involves self-discovery and healing. This personal journey can be supported by:

- **Acknowledging the Shame:** By first admitting the impact of societal messages, it becomes clear that shame is not a compulsion but rather a social construct imposed upon us, and it is a critical first step. Calling out these feelings helps reduce their power.
- **Finding Affirming Communities:** LGBTQ+ spaces (offline and online) can validate feelings, foster open communication, and help people find resources.

- **Seeking Representation:** By advocating for accurate and fair representation of diverse communities, queer identities can be normalized. This can also help show that there is nothing wrong with being different.
- **Engaging in Activism:** Turning challenges into power is what activism is all about—a beautiful, community-driven act that fosters a sense of agency and pride.
- **Therapeutic Support:** Counselling, therapy, and other forms of support can help individuals process their emotions in a healthy manner.

Celebrating Pride

Pride should also be celebrated in everyday life, that too, beyond parades and festivals. By living authentically, showing joy, and building bridges and communities, we can honor the struggles of past generations.

In the end, reclaiming identity is an act of defiance against a world that often marginalizes queer individuals. It is a scream into the wind that all lives are valuable and worthy of being celebrated every day. The transition from shame to pride may not be linear; however, it contributes to creating a freer and more accepting generation. We must work towards a world where anyone can look into a mirror and feel pride, not shame.

– Hidden Wounds: Bullying in Indian Schools –

When we think of schools, we all envision hundreds of children, diverse in color, shape, size, race, and ethnicity, walking through the hallways, bound together by school uniforms adorned with the school's crest. These uniforms, while intended to foster a sense of equality, often fail to create genuine belonging within students, which can even cause dysphoria for many gender non-conforming ones, all bound by groupism, unrealistic standards, and so-called "popularity". In today's day and age, wearing the same name on your back cannot overcome the stigma around simple differences. But this is not just about uniforms; it is about belonging.

Imagine being a teenager, in middle or high school, navigating an environment that is intended for learning and building skills, but which can also be toxic and deeply discriminatory. In many Indian schools, bullying is a major issue, particularly for those who are perceived as different, whether it be for how they look or what they like. If you do not conform to their norms, you are a target. If you do not express yourself like them, you are a target. If you are just a bit different, you are a target. This constant nagging extends beyond the student body and often includes the educators themselves, who sometimes spare no opportunity to hurl cutting remarks. All this adds up to a student's self-esteem crumbling, especially without a strong support system.

Consider the story of Rohan (name changed for anonymity), a student from Delhi, who shared his story. "Every day felt like a battle," he recalled, and nothing less can be said about his experience. Teachers would make snide comments about his appearance and interests. During recess, instead of socializing with his peers, he would hide in the washroom, avoiding the torment. However, this narrative is not limited to him. According to a 2018 survey by the Centre for Civil Society, over 40% of students in Indian schools reported bullying, primarily with perceived differences as the reason.

The impact of such an environment is profound within school communities. Students who are here to learn and build friendships often end up excluding their peers. Educators, who are tasked with nurturing young minds, often contribute to the hostile atmosphere, leaving students like Rohan feeling isolated and hopeless. They claim the problem lies within the bullied students, suggesting they are unable to make friends. But have they ever considered the environment they have created?

Bullying in Indian schools is a pressing issue that demands urgent attention. Creating a safe and inclusive environment should be a priority, where every student, regardless of their differences, feels valued and accepted. By working collaboratively with schools, students, and educators, we can mitigate this issue. Only then can we hope to nurture a generation that is empathetic, inclusive, and resilient, where all hidden wounds are healed.

– Bridging Identities: Intersectionality in the – LGBTQ+ Community

You may have heard of the term **'The Wheel of Power'** before, and in simple terms, it highlights the biases and discrimination in society today. Essentially, it classifies how specific parameters equate to more privilege for a person. It falls under categories of groups that hold power and those that are marginalized, based on parameters such as language, wealth, citizenship, color, sexuality, and other factors. Now, let's say you identify yourself as a member of the LGBTQ+ community but are also not fluent in English, have some form of disability, and are a person of color. That is what you would call intersectionality — a complex blend of various marginalized identities that can overlap to create more discrimination for an individual. Fundamentally, the struggles of queer people are further amplified in numerous ways when they are part of other communities.

- **Cultural Context:** Various communities and cultures may have different perspectives on the queer community, which can, in turn, make a queer person's journey more challenging. According to the Pew Research Center, only 7% of Nigerians accept this community compared to 85% of Canadians.
- **Disability:** People who have disabilities usually face more prejudice and stereotyping. That, paired with being part of the LGBTQ+ community, which may also face discrimination, creates more struggle. Not all Pride Events can include accommodation for all sorts of disabilities, thus, not allowing them to empower themselves or others like them.
- **Socio-economic Status:** Queer people may find it harder to earn income, find housing, and more. People who are from a lower monetary and educational background and are also queer may find it harder to find jobs that accept their identities and qualifications. Furthermore, they can also struggle to find housing, once again, due to discrimination, especially youth who are often rejected by their family.

Above are only a few of the many intersectional fields, and the categories into which people can fall are broader and host different barriers. Intersectional LGBTQ+ individuals with multiple identities can lead to more obstacles in areas like healthcare, employment, and social acceptance, but we as individuals can take small steps to help them. This involves educating ourselves and those around us, advocating for inclusive policies, amplifying and supporting smaller voices, and being supportive allies.

In the end, whether you are a queer black woman or a trans wheelchair user, bridging your identities and accepting each and every one is essential to breaking down the wheel of power and empowering the intersectional.

– Beyond Labels: –
Gender-Neutral Washrooms for All

School is the first major step a child takes out of their comfort zone, stepping from the familiar safety of home into a broader social world. It is a place where they learn not just academics but also navigate social structures, many of which are fraught with challenges. One of the significant yet often overlooked issues is the use of gendered washrooms. And something as simple as a washroom can make all the difference. Gender-neutral washrooms are essential, providing everyone with a safe space, regardless of their gender identity.

Just imagine a young child stepping into a school washroom, only to feel a sense of dread. For many LGBTQIA+ students, this is not an occasional discomfort but a daily battle. A study conducted by the Indian Institute of Management Ahmedabad (IIM-A) found that 62% of transgender students in Indian schools experience verbal or physical harassment due to the lack of gender-neutral facilities. 60% of transgender people in the US avoid public bathrooms for fear of being harassed.

Gender-neutral washrooms provide a straightforward and practical solution to a complex issue. Not every student fits neatly into the categories of 'male' or 'female.' For instance, consider a young gay boy, a trans or non-binary kid, who feels uncomfortable in a boys' bathroom due to fear of being bullied or being misunderstood. They, like many others, would find solace in a gender-neutral option, where the anxiety of fitting in is alleviated. By implementing gender-neutral washrooms, schools can foster a more inclusive and welcoming environment. This can be achieved by converting existing single-stall restrooms or designating some multi-stall washrooms for all genders, ensuring they are private and safe for the personal identities of students.

However, this progressive step has not been without controversy. The National Commission for Protection of Child Rights (NCPCR) criticized a manual released by the National Council of Educational Research and Training (NCERT) in November, which suggested introducing gender-neutral toilets and uniforms in schools. The NCPCR argued that such measures could cause "unnecessary psychological trauma" and "deprivation of equal rights" to children, pointing out the mismatch with children's "gender realities and basic needs." Following this, the manual was pulled down from the NCERT website.

Yet, one must question the rationale behind such resistance. Is it truly about protecting children's rights, or is it about maintaining a status quo that resists acknowledging the diversity of gender identities? By shying away from providing safe spaces like gender-neutral washrooms, is it not the students' right to safety and their dignity being denied? The NCPCR's stance, while cloaked in concern, inadvertently perpetuates a culture of exclusion and stigma.

In a world that is rapidly evolving, our educational systems must not lag behind. They must reflect and embrace the diversity of the society they serve. Gender-neutral washrooms are not just about infrastructure; they are about sending a message of acceptance and equality. It is time to move beyond outdated binaries and recognize the spectrum of identities that exist within our schools. As educators, parents, and policymakers, we must ask ourselves: Are we creating an environment that supports all students, or are we complicit in a system that marginalizes the vulnerable? The answer to this question will define the kind of society we are building for the future.

– Queer Representation in Media –

In today's ever-evolving world, media and television play an influential role in our day-to-day lives. From pop culture to raving about the next season of a well-loved series, it holds power, which, when used to one's advantage, can spread awareness and shape others' perceptions. But for the LGBTQIA+ community, media is more than just that. It is a platform to show others, like them, who are well-known and widely loved.

And it does not end there; it is scientifically proven by surveys and experiments. A survey by GLADD and P&G in 2020 found that queer representation increased by 45%. And complexities can be broken down too; seeing things in a normal light normalizes them. Just as going to school each day has become normal over time since your first day, seeing queer characters on screen regularly will normalize their presence and acceptance, thereby taking a step toward destigmatizing the community.

With this, the LGBTQIA+ community will be seen and heard. However, it is also imperative to consider the layered complexity of identities when attempting to represent them. Including only white, well-off, gay men will not make the cut. Curating a blend of different ethnicities, races, cultures, sizes, disabilities, and more is what will bring the true essence of representation, especially in the media, where many minorities have been advocating for their presence. (Take a look at our previous blog on intersectionality to know more about the depth of a person's identity.)

However, how the queer community is represented in the media also affects its perception. As for yourself, is the representation you see on TV realistic, accurate, relatable, and diverse? Let's take a look at how queer representation appears in media and its various types.

No Representation

More like the absence of representation, many shows show no queer people, or sometimes characters with no diversity at all. I do not think you can find any LGBTQIA+ characters in franchises like Jurassic Park. In addition, many countries, such as Singapore, are notorious for censoring queer media.

Negative Representation

Negative representation usually revolves around stereotypes, prejudice, and preconceived notions. All this can harm members of the community by perpetuating stereotypes. An example is the show "Orange is the New Black", where it is not directly mentioned, but lines such as the character calling herself a lesbian turn straight imply that there is no in between straight and gay, not considering bisexuality.

Positive Representation

Positive representation openly accepts and realistically depicts queer characters, which audiences have come to know and love. It helps destigmatize the community and build awareness. An idealistic representation would be one where a character's problems do not revolve around queerness, although it is not widely seen.

This article only covers a few of the ways the community is represented in the media. Other ways are queerbaiting, token representation, retroactive representation, and more, and all of them have different impacts. It will take time to fully master representation because identities are complex and multifaceted, but while we wait, it is best to appreciate all the unique characteristics of individuals, queer or not. In the end, it is the steps taken to foster acceptance that can truly help advocate for LGBTQIA+ representation in media, television, on the big screen, or even in a small alleyway where everyone gathers to watch a show on their communal TV.

– The Forgotten Connection between Mythology – and LGBTQ+

Love, in its purest form, transcends all barriers. It is a force that defies societal norms, cultures, and prejudices. Yet, in our modern world, we often claim the existence of the LGBTQ community to be a Western influence or an imposed external disease. People against the LGBTQ community suggest that this community is 'against Indian culture'. But is it really true? The *Kama Sutra,* written in the 4th century AD, openly discusses physical pleasure in male-male unions. It vividly details the experiences and pleasures of same-sex relationships, showing that such unions were acknowledged and accepted in ancient times. This ancient text, far from condemning these practices, integrated them into the broader spectrum of human sexuality.

In Valmiki's *Ramayana,* Hanuman observed Rakshasa women kissing and embracing each other, a clear depiction of same-sex affection. Another poignant tale from the *Ramayana* is that of King Dilip's two wives, who, following his death, were instructed by Lord Shiva to make love to each other to conceive a child, which later resulted in the birth of Bhagiratha.

In the *Mahabharata,* Shikhandi, the daughter of King Drupada, was raised as a prince and married to a woman. This narrative not only highlights gender fluidity but also the acceptance of same-sex unions.

In 1860, Thomas Macaulay introduced Section 377, criminalizing same-sex relations and marking a shift from India's earlier acceptance. Victorian sensibilities were shocked by India's openness to sexuality, leading Indian nationalists to adopt conservative attitudes to assert cultural respectability. By the time Deepa Mehta's film *Fire* was released in 1998, depicting a lesbian relationship, Indian society had been conditioned to view homosexuality as unnatural. The backlash was severe, with political bodies vehemently protesting against what they claimed was an "alien" concept.

Art and literature from various periods in Indian history, such as the sculptures in the Puri Jagannath Temple, also depict homosexuality. Poets like Insha and Rangin openly wrote about same-sex relationships in the 1800s, treating them as natural as any other form of love.

After all these examples, shall we continue debating that fighting for the LGBTQ is an 'American Game'? Are we still not convinced that this part of our society was reserved as power and beauty? So, when did things change?

We are all required to pay heed to our age-old learnings and history because this is the only way culture and the modern world can integrate.

– Discovering Self: How Online Communities – Shape LGBTQIA+ Youth in India Amid the Digital Chaos

Quiet of the night, when the world remains silent, many LGBTQIA+ youth worldwide turn to their screens. It is in these quiet moments, where the only light is the soft glow of a phone or laptop, that young people from small towns to sprawling metros seek out communities where they feel seen—where their identity is not something to be hidden but celebrated.

Growing up in India, where societal norms can be rigid, it is not uncommon for LGBTQIA+ youth to feel suffocated by the expectations placed on them. Conversations about gender and sexuality are often wrapped in layers of stigma, or worse, met with silence. And yet, in this very environment, the internet has emerged as a lifeline—a place where identities can be explored and embraced without the immediate fear of backlash.

Take, for instance, platforms like Tumblr, Instagram, and dedicated LGBTQIA+ groups on Facebook. They are more than just websites—they are gateways to a world where 'normal' is not defined by heteronormative standards. Here, young people find others who understand their journey, who have walked similar paths, who have wrestled with the same questions and fears. It is in these spaces that a young person in, say, Lucknow, might first encounter terms like 'genderfluid' or 'asexual,' realizing that they are not alone, and more importantly, that they are valid.

In a 2020 survey conducted by the Gaylaxy Magazine, a staggering 87% of LGBTQIA+ youth in India reported that online communities were their primary source of information and support regarding their sexuality and gender identity (Gaylaxy Magazine, 2020). This statistic highlights a reality that is both empowering and concerning. Empowering, because it shows how crucial these spaces are in helping young people understand themselves; concerning, because it also reveals how much traditional sources—schools, families, media—are failing in this regard.

Yet, the internet is a double-edged sword. While it offers a sanctuary, it is also rife with dangers. The anonymity that protects a closeted teen can just as easily hide a predator or a bully. In India, where cyber laws are still catching up with the times, LGBTQIA+ youth are especially vulnerable. A report by the Internet Freedom Foundation found that nearly 60% of LGBTQIA+ individuals in India had experienced some form of online harassment, ranging from hate speech to threats of violence (Internet Freedom Foundation, 2021).

Ritika, a 17-year-old from a conservative family in Bhopal, shares her experience: "I found an amazing community online where I could talk about my feelings. But then, I started getting messages from strangers, some of them really nasty. They would say horrible things because I was bisexual. It made me scared to even open my phone."

The sad truth is that while online spaces can be liberating, they can also be terrifying. For every supportive message, there might be a dozen slurs waiting in the inbox. This duality is what makes navigating the digital landscape such a fraught experience for LGBTQIA+ youth.

So, how do we ensure these young people can explore their identities without falling into the dark corners of the web? It starts with awareness—parents, educators, and community leaders must understand the importance of these online spaces while also recognizing the risks involved. Digital literacy programs need to be implemented not only in cities, but also in rural areas, where access to safe spaces may be even more limited.

There is also a need for stronger regulations. Cyberbullying laws in India, though existent, are not always enforced with the rigor they require. Activists have long called for more specific protections for LGBTQIA+ individuals, who are often targeted for their sexual orientation or gender identity. Until these protections are in place, the onus, unfortunately, falls on users themselves to safeguard their digital identities.

But this is not just about avoiding harm—it is about thriving. LGBTQIA+ youth deserve to flourish in spaces where they feel at home, where their identities can be celebrated rather than ridiculed. Initiatives like Queerala's online workshops and the Nazariya Foundation's virtual support groups are already creating safer, more affirming spaces for young people to connect. These efforts are vital, but they need to be scaled up and supported at every level of society.

– On The Shelf: The Importance of Queer – Representation in Literature

I am sure we have all made a choice to pick up a book at least once in our lives, whether to get lost in a science-fiction novel at 3 in the morning, or to reminisce about the time when we were not glued to our phones. The truth being, books play a huge role in shaping our perceptions, even if we are not avid readers. Someone or the other has definitely read a book and ranted to you about it (I am that friend), or you might have read a book for school. Essentially, books have always been a powerful medium for exploring human experiences, identities, and imaginations.

And how does this relate to queer representation? Since books play such a prominent role in our lives, whatever we read is deeply embedded in our understanding and opinions.

For LGBTQIA+ members, when they are represented in literature, they feel validated and seen, and it brings normalization to the community. For others, it is embedded into their understanding, thus making positive representation imperative for fostering acceptance.

The Importance of Queer Representation in Literature

- Validation: When books feature characters who are similar to oneself, it makes a person feel seen and understand that they are not alone.
- Expanding Perspectives: Diverse narratives can challenge stereotypes, break down prejudices, and foster empathy.
- Creating Safe Spaces: Queer readers may find solace in books where their experiences are reflected, especially if treated with respect.

Today, there are numerous accomplished authors who have released books related to queer identities, such as Casey McQuiston and Becky Albertalli. Some of my favorites are Adam Silvera's "They Both Die at the End" and "More Happy Than Not". And what is truly great about these books is that I did not pick them up because they featured LGBTQIA+ inclusion, but because the storyline and plot were appealing, regardless of the type of relationship. That is what will encourage readers of all sexualities to pick up these books. But, despite the progress, there are still gaps in queer representation that need to be addressed.

What We Need

- Variety of Genres: LGBTQIA+ stories need to extend beyond romances and coming-of-age stories. We need narratives where being queer is not the focus but just an additional piece of their identity. Maybe a story about an accomplished scientist on their way to the other side of the universe who just so happens to be queer.

- Intersectional Representation: Stories need to consider all aspects of a person's identity. We need characters that are diverse in more than one way.
- More Narratives: We need to expand beyond just relationships in stories. It is time to look at job opportunities, healthcare, education and more.

In conclusion, Queer Representation in books is more than just a trend. Books have the power to write our stories and change them, making it essential to have realistic and diverse representation. We are on the path to do so, but we still need to do some work, and by reading and promoting books that have true LGBTQIA+ representation, we can do our part in the same. So, the next time you go to the bookstore, take a look at a few Queer representing books.

– Threads of Identity: Fashion's Role in Accepting – Your Identity

For most of us, clothes are simply a few threads stitched together to wear. For others, they serve as a way to keep up with trends and step out of their comfort zone. But for the queer community, fashion transcends mere utility. It becomes a statement of individuality and a powerful method of communication. In the LGBTQIA+ community, fashion is one of the most effective tools for challenging societal norms through visible expression. Whether it is a few rainbows here and there or wearing clothes "meant" for another gender, each piece holds its own story of an individual's journey of self-discovery.

Individuality in Fashion

For many people, fashion can feel restrictive. Historically, clothing items were designed for specific audiences—dresses for girls, suits for boys, pink for girls, blue for boys. These categories impose limits on personal identity, sending a message to many young people that they need to fit into a specific mold. However, breaking these boundaries and exploring clothing—even if it was not "meant" for you—allows individuals to express themselves as they truly are. For the queer community, this is a step toward self-acceptance, wearing what feels authentic. Every piece of clothing is deliberately curated to affirm one's identity.

Fashion for Communication

Fashion serves as a silent yet loud tool for self-expression, allowing individuals to share their identity without uttering a word. Take Pride parades, for example—every outfit tells a story, has meaning, and serves a purpose. For members of the LGBTQIA+ community, even the smallest hint of a subtle pattern can become a catalyst for self-acceptance and a way to proclaim that acceptance to the world. It is the women shouting, "I can wear a suit and tie too!" It is the men shouting, "I can wear pink and frilly outfits too!" It is the queer community shouting, "I don't have to wear what you wear!"

Challenging Stereotypes

By stepping outside of boundaries assigned by society, queer fashion challenges and transforms societal norms. It questions what is considered normal and accepted. In the end, what will happen if a man wears a dress? It opens a whole new pathway to that person's journey of expressing their true self. The queer community's embrace of diverse and flexible styles is a breath of fresh air, challenging rigid expectations.

Ultimately, fashion, clothing, and even accessories play a crucial role in accepting diverse identities. As a catalyst for change and a platform for self-expression, it is a tool that has the power to transform lives.

– Foreign Influence: Role of the World in – Indian Society

For years, people have believed that the LGBTQIA+ community in India is some sort of "Western influence." But when we dive into our history and mythology, a different picture emerges—one where gender fluidity and same-sex love have always been part of our culture. Our mythology is filled with stories where gender was not a strictly binary concept. And if you thought *Lihaaf* by Ismat Chugtai was bold, imagine what social media would have said back in the day!

Blame the British (Again!)

While India was once open about gender and sexuality, the British arrived and, well, messed up our mindset. In 1861, they introduced Section 377, a law that basically said, "No more fun, love only happens one way!" This law pushed the

LGBTQIA+ community into the shadows and began a long period of pretending things did not exist.

The Fight for Equality

In the 2000s, things started heating up (not just because of climate change). The Naz Foundation challenged Section 377, and in 2009, the Delhi High Court decriminalized homosexuality. However, the excitement was short-lived—much like when our Wi-Fi cuts out during a binge session. In 2013, the Supreme Court reinstated Section 377, pushing the LGBTQIA+ community back into the shadows.

Fast forward to 2018, and after years of resilience and activism, the Supreme Court finally got it right. The criminalization of same-sex relationships was struck down, and it was a *yass queen* moment for the LGBTQIA+ community.

Six Years Later: So, What's the Tea?

It has been six years since that victory, and although same-sex love is no longer a crime, the journey is not over. LGBTQIA+ couples still cannot get married, making the dream of a big fat Indian wedding seem distant. On the plus side, you can now open a joint bank account with your partner!

Corporate India

While the legal system is still dragging its feet, corporate India seems to be catching up. Some companies are offering insurance benefits for queer partners, and workplaces are beginning to adopt gender-sensitivity programs. However, we are still waiting for those gender-neutral washrooms.

The Road Ahead for Us

For our generation, it is about more than just laws—it is about changing mindsets. Whether it is showing up for Pride, creating LGBTQIA+ safe spaces in schools, or calling out that one friend who still thinks it is okay to make lame homophobic jokes, we have a big role to play.

As we celebrate six years since the decriminalization of same-sex love, let's remember this is not just about legal wins—it is about everyday acceptance and creating a future where everyone can be themselves, no filter needed!

– Calling Out vs. Calling In: What to Do? –

I would like to start this blog with a personal anecdote. As a student, I encounter a lot of harmful language used by my peers in an ignorant, FOMO manner. An example of this was when the term 'Gay', which means a person attracted to another person of the same sex, was used as a derogatory term. I found this very offensive. Multiple times, I called out the perpetrators in the conversation, telling them what they were doing was wrong, with no avail. However, it was when I talked to them in private that I began to see change.

So that brings me to this topic. How do we know what to call out, versus what to call in? Which is appropriate for the scenario? How do we get people to listen to us?

Calling Out vs. Calling In!

To call someone out means giving a public response that holds someone responsible for harmful phrases or actions they may have committed.

Meanwhile, to call someone in is when you talk to someone privately, alone, and inform them that what they did was wrong and could hurt people.

When calling in, you may choose to react with curiosity instead of humiliating or shaming the other person. Talking to someone privately gives you the opportunity to get to them, without making them defensive and unresponsive to anything you may tell them. This approach is commonly used when you think a person may not be aware of their actions and their impact.

On the other hand, calling out is when you publicly, in the moment, stop the conversation and point out that the offending phrase or action was harmful and should be addressed. Calling out normally occurs when calling in is not possible and when immediate action is necessary to remedy the situation. It can also happen when the person is aware of their impact, which needs to be mitigated. It can also be used when someone is consistently causing harm.

When to Call out?

You can call someone out when:

- They are openly using hateful, homophobic, or transphobic language, which may have an immediate impact on any recipient.
- Their behavior can harm people (physically or mentally) if left unchecked/unchallenged.
- The person is in a position of power and needs to be held accountable for their actions.

How to Call Someone out?

Some starters you can use to politely call someone out are:

- I'm sorry, I need to interject here.
- Excuse me, I would like to say, as your peer/college/conversationalist, what you are saying can be harmful.
- I cannot continue to be in this meeting/gathering if we continue discussing [insert topic] this way.
- This is the [number of times] you have done this, and it is really harming our community and friends.

  If they ignore, you can always be less nice about it.

When to Call in?

You can call someone in when:

- The person seems unaware of their actions.
- They may be open to discussion and amend their mistakes.
- They may get defensive in the scenario of a public confrontation.

How to Call Someone in?

Some starters you can use to call someone in are:

- I would like to bring up the conversation we were having.
- I am not sure if you know, but what you did…
- I would like to bring up [insert topic] that you mentioned. What did you mean by that?

If this does not work, you can call them out the next time they do this.

Navigating Difficult Conversations:

- Stay calm: It is easy to get angry, but causing a scene will not get anyone anywhere.

- Use "I" statements: Pinning the blame on others may put them on the defensive.
- Be reflective: Ask them to think about the impact of their actions.

Remember, it can be difficult to confront people, but it is essential to address the issue if someone is causing harm. There is a theory that says, in the majority of scenarios, harm is caused by incompetence rather than malicious intent.

– Coming Out and Self-Acceptance –

Personal Journeys and Navigating Societal Pressures

Did you know 45% of LGBTQIA+ youth seriously considered committing suicide in the past year, but those who have accepting families are significantly less likely to attempt it? (The Trevor Project, 2023) Or that 57% of LGBTQIA+ adults, who were rejected by family members, experienced long-term mental health struggles as a result? (PFLAG, 2022)

These are all instances of people who have come out to their friends or families and faced consequences which should not exist. Coming out remains a scary and significant milestone for so many people, simply because of the reaction they think they will get.

Why Is Coming out Still Such a Big Deal?

There are many reasons why coming out to people, even those you trust, is a significant deal.

To begin with, there are safety concerns which need to be considered. LGBTQIA+ people may fear coming out for the fear of being rejected, bullied, or even experiencing violent actions. They may feel the need to assess their environment and peers/family before coming out, to evaluate a supportive environment over a hostile one. Legal protections are still underway, and not very developed in some areas. For example, in Tennessee, a proposed law would allow public school teachers to refuse to call transgender students by their chosen name or pronouns without consequences. However, on the other hand, a Massachusetts policy states that school personnel should use students' chosen names and pronouns that are appropriate to a student's gender identity, regardless of their assigned birth sex.

Moreover, the support networks and acceptance of family and friends also play a large role. Someone may fear rejection from their family and/or friends/loved ones, and these individuals play a huge role in shaping someone's coming-out journey. As seen in the statistic above, supportive environments drastically reduce the chances of LGBTQIA+ members committing suicide. There are also numerous societies that have been established to support the LGBTQIA+ community, for example, GLAAD, The Trevor Project, and PFLAG (including our own *Astitva*).

Societal Pressure

Many LGBTQIA+ individuals may also fear rejection due to cultural and religious beliefs or societal pressures, which may conflict with their unique identity. Different communities perceive LGBTQIA+ individuals in different ways. However, it is important to consider that several religions and histories have supported LGBTQIA+ individuals. In Hinduism, there are several texts that refer to a third gender, apart from male or female. Further back, in Greek, Roman, and Norse

Mythology, several gods and humans were referred to as homosexual, asexual and gender-fluid.

However, we also need to consider societal biases and depictions of normal. Many people still follow typical gender norms, and upon experiencing homo- or transphobia, may lead people to doubt themselves and their own gender identity. Moreover, there are several reports of LGBTQIA+ discrimination in the workplace or in organizations.

Self-Acceptance (Everything happens at your pace)

Remember, there is no right time to come out. You do not need to assign a label to yourself, and you can do anything at your own pace or your own comfort. You do not need to reveal yourself to everyone, and it is okay to keep your identity private. If you remember who you are, and no matter what anyone else says, nothing can change that.

Get inspired by reading stories, watching films, talking to people, and internalizing their experiences. Forget the hate and the stigma and find your own role models. Start journaling and find a community; there are people everywhere. Confide in someone you trust.

– Family and Acceptance –

Undeniably, family plays a significant role in shaping our identity and culture. Our families are the ones to teach us right from wrong, love us, and raise us; they are our first teachers. So, naturally, one would want their family's acceptance and support over all others when coming out or being a part of the LGBTQIA+ community. In fact, acceptance vs. rejection by family for LGBTQIA+ individuals can have a significant impact on their mental health and well-being.

Why Does Familial Acceptance Matter?

Families play such a big role in the mental and physical well-being of LGBTQIA+ individuals. Studies have shown that LGBTQIA+ individuals show physical and mental risks, such as depression, suicidal thoughts, substance abuse, psychological distress, low self-esteem, and others. Studies have also shown that children who were rejected by their parents were even more susceptible to these risks.

Most families with ambivalent or negative views about sexual minorities still love their children, and believe they are helping them to fit in and thrive by rejecting their sexual orientation and/or gender identities. Yet, such families have been shown to successfully modify their behavior when they learn how harmful rejecting behavior can be to their children's mental and physical health.

Coming out to your family is an important part of your healthy development, and in the long term can reduce the stress associated with worrying about future rejection; however, research shows that the short-term effects of coming out can include added stress resulting from social isolation and family conflict, particularly if your parents react in rejecting ways.

What Are Challenges Faced by Families?

There are so many challenges that families may face when an LGBTQIA+ individual is coming out to them. For example, they may reject their child due to social expectations and the way they have been taught things. As mentioned above, they may reject their child out of fear that they will not fit into society and, by extension, not thrive in it.

There may also be some generational gap, which may hinder parents' understanding of gender and sexuality, as education about such topics then was very different from now. They may also fear judgment from their extended family or other loved ones.

Family background, including race, class, ethnicity, religion, national and regional origin and other factors, can play a role in shaping how parents and youth respond to LGBT identity.

How Can Families Support Their Children?

According to research by the Family Acceptance Project, families can support their LGBTQIA+ children by affirming their sexual orientation and gender expression, talking with children about their LGBTQIA+ identity, defending them when experiencing peer victimization, connecting them to an LGBTQIA+ role model, and welcoming their LGBTQIA+ peers into the home. Research suggests that the number and quality of accepting behaviors matters to youth well-being.

Families are not perfect each time. However, it is important to educate yourselves about the LGBTQIA+ community and be understanding and supportive if a family member comes out to you.

– Self-Acceptance and Empathy –

According to the dictionary definition, self-acceptance refers to satisfaction or fulfilment with oneself, while empathy means the ability to understand and feel another's feelings.

These two concepts are deeply entwined in the concept of LGBTQIA+ individuals. We need to achieve self-acceptance, and the road to self-acceptance is through empathy. It is hard to affirm ourselves when no one else does.

The Journey to Self-Acceptance

- The first step to self-acceptance is to understand that it is okay to be outside the norm. You need to overcome your internalized stigma and the impact of societal pressures, and simply be yourself.
- You need to break free from expectations. You cannot accept yourself if you are constantly trying to measure up to someone else's standards for you.
- Understand that your identity is a beautiful thing, and no one can take it from you. It is yours, forever.
- You need to understand that just because you are LGBTQIA+, it does not mean you will have a different life. Many people before you and many after you will continue to live happy, successful lives. So, what is stopping you?

Role of Empathy

- Surrounding yourself with empathetic people is crucial in achieving self-acceptance. They are there to affirm your worth to you when you are questioning it yourself.

- You can also find acceptance in shared experiences. Listening to someone else who has gone through the same thing may help you find your own self-acceptance.
- You can also practice empathy towards others. Spreading compassion to others can also make you feel good about yourself and affirm your identity.

How to Build Self-Acceptance and Empathy

- Positive Self-Talk and Affirmations: Remind yourself about your worth and your importance.
- Surround Yourself with Supportive People: They are there to pick you up on your darkest days.

Self-Acceptance is an ongoing process, not a one-time achievement. Practice empathy towards yourself and towards others, and remember, there is only one you, and that you is amazing, and people love them, and you should too.

– Understanding Identities: – Breaking down Gender, Sex, and Sexualities

Let me ask you a question: When someone says gender, what does it mean to you? If I ask you to give me a synonym for 'gender,' what will you say? Are 'gender' and 'sex' the same thing? What about sexuality? Where does that come in? These are three different words which are often used interchangeably and without much thought behind them. But these three terms, similar as they may be, are not the same.

Let me define for you: **What is Gender, what is Sex, and what is Sexuality.**

What is Gender: Gender, fundamentally, is a social construct used to classify a person as a man, woman, non-binary, or any other identity. Your gender does not have to identify with whichever gender you were identified with at birth, based on your organs.

There are several categories of gender identity, a few of which may include, cisgender (where your gender identifies with the one assigned at birth), transgender (where you do not identify with your gender assigned at birth), non-binary (where you may feel both, or neither male or female), or queer/questioning (where your gender identity falls outside of the societal norm).

What is Sex: Your sex, in short, is the gender you were assigned at birth, based on your organs or external anatomy. Your sex is totally independent of your gender, and you may or may not identify with the sex you were assigned. Normally, sex is binary, male or female; however, in some cases, sex can be varied, such as intersex (people born with a variety of sex traits and/or reproductive anatomy).

What is Sexuality: Your sexuality is a sum of your entire identity. It defines your sex, your gender, and your sexual orientation, or who you may love or be attracted to (if any). Your sexuality is basically your personal identity card, and it does not need to fit any labels.

Your Sexuality Is Yours

To conclude, the terms gender, sex, and sexuality are all very different. They correspond to a different part of your identity, and all are worth acknowledging. And remember, your identity is not set in stone.

– What to Do If a Friend Comes Out to You? –

Okay, so it is a big moment. Your friend has come out to you. This person can be your best friend, your family member, a loved one, or even an acquaintance. The point is, this person trusts you and has told you about their sexuality. So, here is the million-dollar question. What do you say?

What to Do?

- Listening Is Key: One of the biggest things about being an ally is realizing that these moments are not about you. Your friend probably just needs an ear, someone to depend on. It has everything to do with listening to your friend without judgment.
- Ask Your Friend What They Need: Sometimes, all people need is a listening ear. And if your friend needs that, it is great! Give it to them. But sometimes they may want support, or advice, or anything else. Make sure to be supportive and affirmative with them.
- Thank Them for Trusting You: Deciding to share their identity with you is a significant step for most people. Make sure to thank them for trusting you and show your support. Chances are that your friend is nervous about how you will take it. Show them that there is no reason to be afraid, and you will support them regardless.

- Affirm Their Identity: Use their correct name/pronouns (in case of gender); if you misgender them, apologize.

What NOT to Do?

- Don't Make It a Big Deal: Surely, you may want to ask a billion questions to your friend, but the important thing is to act like and feel like nothing has changed. And really, nothing has changed. Your friend is still the same person. It can mean so much to them if you still treat them as you would normally.
- Don't Invalidate Their Experience: Do not ask them questions such as "Are you sure?" or say, "It's just a phase." These statements are incredibly harmful to their mental health, and they may feel unsure about their own identity.
- Don't Make It about You: This is not a time to share your own opinion and experience, especially if they are experiencing something you have not. This is about them, not you.
- Don't out Them: Do not, EVER, out your friend to other people. They have trusted you with their secret, and they may not be comfortable with you telling other people about it. Not to mention, it can actually harm them by inviting bullies and/or homo- trans-phobic people.

How to Support Your Friend beyond the Moment?

- Respect Their Pace: Do not pressure your friend to do something they are not ready for. Let them take things as slowly as they want to.

- Educate Yourself: Learn about the LGBTQIA+ community and the proper terminologies. It is important to know about a subject that may become close to you.
- Be Their Ally: Correct people who misgender them (don't out them! Ask for their consent). Invite them to LGBTQIA+ events and support their rights.
- Check in Regularly: Make sure you are supportive of them and their feelings.

– Understanding Pronouns and Language –

Why Inclusive Language Matters

Why Do Pronouns Matter?

Pronouns are an important part of people's identity. In English and regular usage, they are used to define nouns and also to specify the gender of nouns. Knowing and using people's correct pronouns (which are defined by them) fosters inclusion and makes people feel respected and valued. It also affirms their gender identity.

It is so crucial that people (such as friends, families, or even total strangers), workplaces, and organizations all support a person's use of self-identified first names, even despite any legal names, and self-identified pronouns, which may differ from assumed pronouns at birth or other's perceptions of physical appearance.

How to Introduce Pronouns?

Someone's pronouns should not just be assumed. It is the same as assuming someone's name. You do not know it, so why are you trying to guess?

You can open the portal in the conversation by normalizing the sharing of pronouns. You can also introduce your own pronouns and prompt the other person to do the same. For example, I would say:

Hi! My name is Aanya and I use she/her pronouns.

Alternatively, you can add your pronouns when you are signing your name on a mail, for example:

Best Regards,
NAME (she/her)

Avoid using binary language, such as 'Ladies or Gentlemen', or 'Boys and Girls', but rather use words like 'One and All', or 'Everyone'.

Remember: Do not assume someone's pronouns based on their assigned sex or their appearance. Everyone is diverse.

Why Is This Even Important?

Studies have proven that using other people's correct pronouns and using gender-neutral pronouns is more than important.

Being misgendered and/or misnamed may leave people feeling disrespected, invalidated, or even dismissed. This can threaten people's mental health.

Transgender and non-binary people are twice as likely to have suicidal thoughts as the general population, and are up to four times as likely to engage in risky substance use. Studies have found that when compared with peers who cannot use their chosen name and pronoun, young people who can experience 71% fewer symptoms of severe depression, a 34% decrease in reported thoughts of suicide and a 65% decrease in suicide attempts.

Tips for Getting Pronouns Right

- Don't Assume
- Ask for people's gender pronouns (But avoid doing it publicly)
- Share your own gender pronouns
- Apologize if you misgender someone
- Help others
- Practice!

So, to conclude, I would like to say pronouns are a very integral part of people's identity. I think it is important to remember that it is important to be inclusive.

– Chapter 5 – Infographics

France's LGBTQIA+ Community Still Faces Rising Discrimination and Violence
Despite advances like legalizing same-sex marriage, the LGBTQIA+ community in France continues to experience significant discrimination and violence.
A 2023 report from SOS Homophobie revealed over 1,500 cases of LGBTQIA+ phobia in 2022, including a worrying 28% increase in physical assaults. Much of this discrimination happens in public spaces, online, and even within families, showing how deeply ingrained prejudice against the LGBTQIA+ community remains in parts of French society.
what's happening?
One of the most tragic examples is the case of 13-year-old Lucas, who took his own life in January 2023 after being repeatedly bullied with homophobic insults at school. His death highlights the devastating effects of anti-LGBTQIA+ bullying and how vulnerable young people in the community are to harassment.
While legal progress has been made, including the celebration of a decade of marriage equality, the rise in these violent incidents shows that LGBTQIA+ individuals still face many barriers to living safely and openly.
https://www.lemonde.fr/en/france/article/2023/05/16/french-lgbtq-organization-signals-high-alert-for-homophobic-acts_6026840_7.html# https://www.sos-homophobie.org/
matter

Crisis in Uganda
WHATS HAPPENING IN UGANDA?
The LGBTQIA community in Uganda faces severe threats from the reintroduced Anti-Homosexuality Bill, which could impose a 3-year sentence for failing to report community members
a life sentence for engaging in same-sex relationships, and even the death penalty for "aggravated" offenses. Additionally, providing assistance to LGBTQIA individuals could lead to a 7-year sentence.
This legislation fosters a climate of fear and discrimination, putting activists and health workers at great risk. The situation underscores significant human rights violations, making advocacy and international support crucial for the safety and rights of the LGBTQIA community in Uganda. For more information, visit resources from Human Rights Watch, Amnesty International, OutRight Action International, and ILGA.
RESOURCES
ILGA World - The International Lesbian, Gay, Bisexual, Trans and Intersex Association
Human rights in Uganda Amnesty International
astitva
ASTITVA TEENS

THE FALSE FINES FROM RUSSIA

ASTITVA TEENS
presents

Issues with the Lgbtq in Russia

The LGBTQIA+ community in Russia faces significant challenges due to a proposed anti-gay bill that would ban public events, claiming to protect minors.

This law could impose fines of up to $1,600 for any public expression related to LGBTQIA+ identities.

what do they Experience

The community experiences discrimination and violence, with activists facing legal hurdles and social stigma. Despite international concerns, the Russian government prioritizes traditional values over their rights.

In summary, this proposed law threatens the safety and dignity of the LGBTQIA+ community in Russia, highlighting the need for ongoing advocacy.

LGBTQIA+ Reports in Mexico

whats happening in Mexico?

In Mexico, the LGBTQIA+ communities face significant challenges, including high rates of abuse and harassment. Reports show that around 80% of LGBTQIA+ people experience discrimination, with transgender individuals particularly at risk. In 2020, there were 79 documented murders of LGBTQIA+ people, highlighting the dangers they face. Many do not report these incidents due to fear of being mocked or a lack of trust in law enforcement, which adds to a culture of silence.

law enforcement

While marriage is legal in 27 out of 32 states, some areas still do not recognize these rights, making it hard for couples to get marriage licenses. In 2015, the Supreme Court of Mexico ruled that bans on marriage are unconstitutional, but there are still many administrative hurdles, especially in conservative regions.

This mix of legal progress and ongoing social issues shows the urgent need for continued advocacy and education to create a safer, more accepting environment for LGBTQIA+ communities in Mexico, ensuring their rights and protection from violence and discrimination.

:Human rights in Mexico Amnesty International
ILGA World: welcome! - ILGA World
Home | Outright International

How is Maldives for people traveling who are part of the LGBTQIA+ community?

1. Sharia Law: The Maldives is an Islamic country that follows Sharia Law, which prohibits same-sex relationships and considers them a crime.
2. Punishments: LGBTQIA+ individuals can face severe punishments, including imprisonment, fines, and even capital punishment, making it a high-risk destination.

LGBTQIA+ travelers face a delicate balance when visiting destinations like the Maldives, where forced discreetness is often necessary to navigate the social landscape. Many individuals must be extremely cautious about revealing their sexual orientation or gender identity to avoid attracting unwanted attention or facing potential persecution. This pressure to remain discreet can significantly diminish the travel experience, as authentic self-expression is curtailed. Furthermore, many luxury resorts in the Maldives have policies that are not LGBTQIA+-friendly, with some even openly discriminating against LGBTQIA+ guests. This unwelcoming environment extends beyond the confines of resorts, as the local population generally holds strong conservative attitudes toward LGBTQIA+ individuals. Such sentiments create an atmosphere where travelers may feel unsafe or unwelcome, further complicating their ability to enjoy their vacation. Additionally, the lack of LGBTQIA+-inclusive services and support networks exacerbates these challenges, making it crucial for travelers to conduct thorough research before visiting. As awareness of these issues grows, it is essential for both the tourism industry and local governments to foster a more inclusive environment that respects and celebrates diversity, ensuring that all travelers can experience the beauty of the Maldives without fear or discrimination.

BRAZIL'S LGBTQIA+ PEOPLE

Laws and Policies

1. Same-sex marriage: Same-sex marriage has been legal in Brazil since 2013, when the National Council of Justice ruled that same-sex couples have the right to marry.
2. Anti-discrimination laws: Brazil has several anti-discrimination laws that protect LGBTQIA+ individuals from discrimination in areas such as employment, education, and healthcare.
3. Transgender rights: Brazil has made significant progress in recent years in promoting transgender rights, including the introduction of a national identity document for transgender individuals.
4. Hate crime laws: Brazil has laws that specifically address hate crime against LGBTQIA+ individuals, including the 2019 law that makes homophobia and transphobia crimes.

Organizations that play a critical role for the LGBTQIA+ community

Grupo Gay da Bahia: The Grupo Gay da Bahia is a pioneering LGBTQIA+ organization in Brazil that has been advocating for LGBTQIA+ rights since the 1980s.

ABGLT: The Brazilian Association of Gays, Lesbians, and Transgender People (ABGLT) is one of the largest and most prominent LGBTQIA+ organizations in Brazil.

In conclusion, despite advancements in LGBTQIA+ rights in Brazil, significant challenges persist. High levels of violence and discrimination, particularly in rural and marginalized communities, remain a grave concern. The current conservative government's stance on LGBTQIA+ issues raises fears of further erosion of rights, while limited access to healthcare, especially for HIV/AIDS treatment and mental health support, continues to hinder the well-being of LGBTQIA+ individuals. Addressing these challenges is essential for fostering a more inclusive and equitable society.

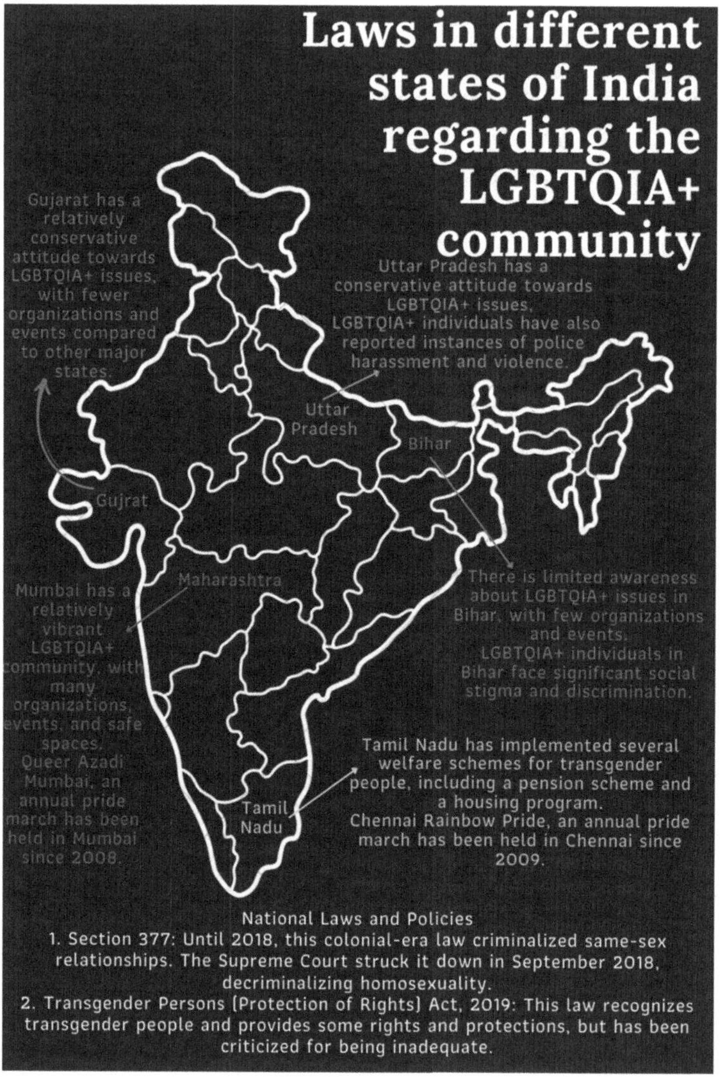
Laws in different states of India regarding the LGBTQIA+ community
Gujarat has a relatively conservative attitude towards LGBTQIA+ issues, with fewer organizations and events compared to other major states.
Gujrat
Uttar Pradesh has a conservative attitude towards LGBTQIA+ issues. LGBTQIA+ individuals have also reported instances of police harassment and violence.
Uttar Pradesh
Bihar
There is limited awareness about LGBTQIA+ issues in Bihar, with few organizations and events. LGBTQIA+ individuals in Bihar face significant social stigma and discrimination.
Maharashtra
Mumbai has a relatively vibrant LGBTQIA+ community, with many organizations, events, and safe spaces. Queer Azadi Mumbai, an annual pride march has been held in Mumbai since 2008.
Tamil Nadu
Tamil Nadu has implemented several welfare schemes for transgender people, including a pension scheme and a housing program. Chennai Rainbow Pride, an annual pride march has been held in Chennai since 2009.
National Laws and Policies
1. Section 377: Until 2018, this colonial-era law criminalized same-sex relationships. The Supreme Court struck it down in September 2018, decriminalizing homosexuality.
2. Transgender Persons (Protection of Rights) Act, 2019: This law recognizes transgender people and provides some rights and protections, but has been criticized for being inadequate.

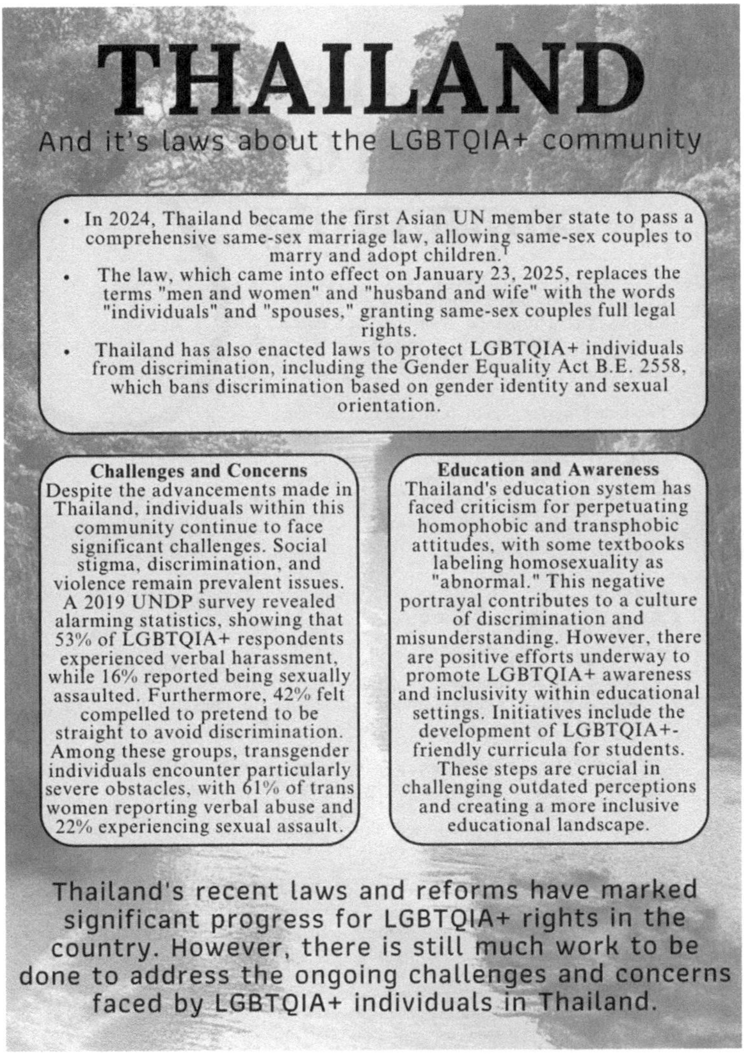
THAILAND
And it's laws about the LGBTQIA+ community
• In 2024, Thailand became the first Asian UN member state to pass a comprehensive same-sex marriage law, allowing same-sex couples to marry and adopt children.[1]
• The law, which came into effect on January 23, 2025, replaces the terms "men and women" and "husband and wife" with the words "individuals" and "spouses," granting same-sex couples full legal rights.
• Thailand has also enacted laws to protect LGBTQIA+ individuals from discrimination, including the Gender Equality Act B.E. 2558, which bans discrimination based on gender identity and sexual orientation.
Challenges and Concerns
Despite the advancements made in Thailand, individuals within this community continue to face significant challenges. Social stigma, discrimination, and violence remain prevalent issues. A 2019 UNDP survey revealed alarming statistics, showing that 53% of LGBTQIA+ respondents experienced verbal harassment, while 16% reported being sexually assaulted. Furthermore, 42% felt compelled to pretend to be straight to avoid discrimination. Among these groups, transgender individuals encounter particularly severe obstacles, with 61% of trans women reporting verbal abuse and 22% experiencing sexual assault.
Education and Awareness
Thailand's education system has faced criticism for perpetuating homophobic and transphobic attitudes, with some textbooks labeling homosexuality as "abnormal." This negative portrayal contributes to a culture of discrimination and misunderstanding. However, there are positive efforts underway to promote LGBTQIA+ awareness and inclusivity within educational settings. Initiatives include the development of LGBTQIA+-friendly curricula for students. These steps are crucial in challenging outdated perceptions and creating a more inclusive educational landscape.
Thailand's recent laws and reforms have marked significant progress for LGBTQIA+ rights in the country. However, there is still much work to be done to address the ongoing challenges and concerns faced by LGBTQIA+ individuals in Thailand.

Iran's take on the LGBTQIA+ community

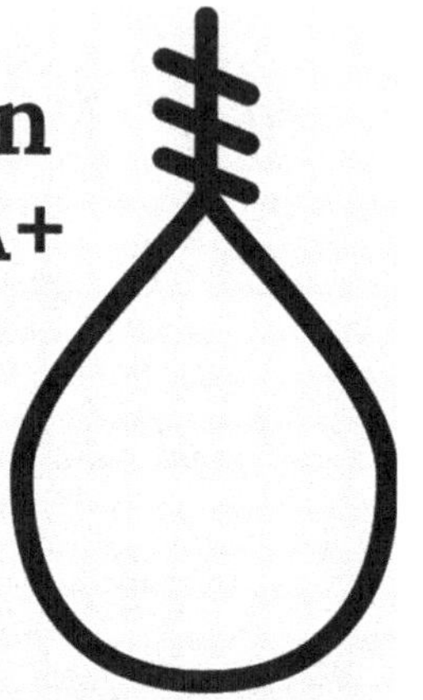

Laws and Punishments

Same-sex relationships are illegal and can be punishable by death, with at least 107 executions recorded between 1979 and 1990.[1]

The death penalty is also applied to those convicted of "sodomy" (lavāt), with both partners potentially facing execution.

Female same-sex activity is punishable by 100 lashes, with the death sentence applicable on the fourth offense.

Myths

Myth 1: LGBTQIA+ individuals are not persecuted in Iran because there are no public executions.

Reality: While public executions are not common, LGBTQIA+ individuals are still persecuted and executed in Iran. Many cases go unreported, and the government often denies or downplays these incidents.

Myth 2: Iran's laws are based on Islamic principles, and therefore, LGBTQIA+ individuals are not protected.

Reality: While Iran's laws are indeed influenced by Islamic principles, many Islamic scholars and interpretations argue that these laws should be reformed to protect the rights of LGBTQIA+ individuals.

Myth 3: The Iranian government is not responsible for the persecution of LGBTQIA+ individuals.

Reality: The Iranian government is directly responsible for the persecution of LGBTQIA+ individuals, through its laws, policies, and actions. The government's rhetoric and actions perpetuate a culture of hate and intolerance.

Part IV
Creative Expression

– Chapter 6 –
Poetry & Creative Expressions

Poetry has always been a powerful vessel for emotions, an outlet for unheard voices, and a mirror reflecting both struggle and resilience. In this chapter, we explore a collection of poems that delve into themes of identity, belonging, pain, and hope—each one a profound expression of human emotions.

- ***One Big Circle*: *A Poem of Belonging*** highlights the silent battles of exclusion and the power of inclusivity. Through simple yet impactful verses, it encourages us to break down barriers and expand our circles, creating spaces where everyone feels seen and valued. It reminds us that true strength lies in unity and that no one should stand alone.
- ***The Fire Within*** is an anthem of resilience, capturing the essence of fighting against adversity. It speaks of overcoming despair, facing fears, and rising from the ashes, much like a phoenix. The poem acknowledges the deep wounds life can leave behind but also celebrates the strength it takes to heal, rebuild, and chase one's dreams relentlessly.
- ***Invisible Voices*** the loneliness of feeling unseen, unheard, and unnoticed. It encapsulates the longing for recognition and the journey toward finding one's place in the world. Through evocative lines, it paints the picture of a soul waiting for its moment to shine—a breeze hoping to become a storm.

- ***Echoes in the Silence*** is a hauntingly raw piece that sheds light on the silent suffering of marginalized youth. It portrays the weight of bullying, rejection, and societal expectations that often drive young souls into darkness. The poem serves as a call to action, urging readers to listen, to care, and to extend kindness before it is too late. It is a voice for those who have been silenced, a reminder that every life deserves to be seen and cherished.

Together, these poems weave a tapestry of emotions that resonate with the struggles and triumphs of those navigating identity, acceptance, and resilience. They remind us that poetry is not just words on a page but a reflection of the world around us—sometimes painful, sometimes hopeful, but always powerful. As you journey through these verses, may you find not just stories, but echoes of your own heart.

One Big Circle: A Poem of Belonging

In a big, big world, where many play,
Some friends join in, some stay away. There's a story, quiet and deep,
Of those who stand alone and seldom leap.

In the field of life, where games are played, not everyone gets to go around.
Some are chosen, some must wait,
Some feel it's luck, some call it fate.

Think of a circle, big and clear,
Where everyone's welcome, far or near.

Yet, outside this ring, some do stand, hoping, wishing, to join the band.
"Why not me?" they often ponder,
As they watch and wait and wonder.
In their hearts, a silent plea, "For once, I wish, they'd pick me."

But what if we changed the way we play,
And made a space where all could stay?
No more "outsiders,"
No more "in,"
Just one big circle, where all fit in.

Let's draw our lines a little wider,
Be the friend, not the divider.
For in a world where we all belong, together, we're unbeaten, bold, and strong.

So, next time you're choosing, look around and see the one who's looking down.
Reach out a hand, pull them through,
For inclusivity starts with you!

- By Medha Matta

The Fire Within

In the depth of night, where shadows blend and weave
Under the moon's light, where many come to grieve
Through storms that rage and wind that tear
Through loss that bends the soul to despair
Not grieve, there isn't a cure
Hits so deep, makes a child mature.
It talks about tough fights and hurts that are real,

About keeping on going, no matter how you feel.

Even when it's easier to just give in,
It says, 'Get back up and fight to win.'
Being brave isn't about not being scared,
It's about facing fear, even when you're unprepared.
It's about fixing what's broken, healing your pain,
And chasing big dreams, again and again.

It is to build from ruins, to heal from scars,
To reach for the moon, to dance with the stars.

It's the spirit of the phoenix, rising from ash,
To resolve and rebuild after each crash,
The ability to laugh, to love, to live,
To take from life's lessons, to grow, and to give.

To the souls who've been broken, yet stand,
Who've walked through the fire, hand in hand,
Guided by their strength, they find their way,
Strong and graceful, nothing makes them sway.

- By Medha Matta

Invisible Voices

So many see me each day, but I never feel seen.
It is something that I hope for, something that I dream.
Thousands have heard my melody, yet I never felt heard.
Every time I tried to speak, everyone replied absurdly.
So many pass by me, yet I feel alone.
I hope that someday, someone will make me feel known.
I'm a breeze in a blow of wind,

Hoping that someday I'll be the storm.

- By Medha Matta

Echoes in the Silence

- Trigger Warning: This poem discusses themes of suicide, bullying, and deep emotional pain. It may be distressing for some readers, especially those who have experienced similar struggles. Please read with care, and if you find yourself affected, consider reaching out to a trusted friend, family member, or mental health professional for support.

The poem delves into the silent torment faced by a young teenager, particularly one who is queer, disabled, or otherwise marginalized. It is a raw and heartfelt expression of the pain and isolation that can come from relentless bullying and societal rejection. The poem is a voice from the beyond, where the child who has taken their own life speaks out, revealing the unbearable weight of their experiences. It is about the desperate need to be seen, loved, and understood, and the tragic consequences when these basic human needs go unmet. Through this piece, I aimed to give a voice to those who are often silenced, shed light on the hidden battles that too many young people face, and urge readers to listen, care, and act before it is too late.

I wasn't always this quiet, you know,
Once had a voice that sang in the flow,
But they told me to hush, to shrink, to hide,
And so I did, with each tear I cried.

The world wasn't built for kids like me,
With bodies too big, or hearts too free,

Or legs that didn't run as fast,
Or love that didn't fit the cast.
They pointed, they laughed, they tore me apart,
Till the seams of my soul unraveled, a start,
Of nights too long, of thoughts too deep,
Of promises broken, of dreams asleep.

I looked in the mirror, searching for truth,
But all I saw was their twisted proof,
That I wasn't enough, that I wasn't right,
So I turned off the switch, extinguished the light.

And now, in the quiet, where no one can hear,
I scream out the pain, I scream out the fear,
Of a world that's cruel, of hearts that don't see
The child inside who just wanted
To be seen, to be loved, to be held close,
Not judged, not pushed, not treated as gross,
Those were the dreams that slipped through my hands,
Like sand in the hourglass, counting demands.
But hear me now, as I fade away,
This wasn't a choice, it wasn't my way,
But the walls were too high, the voices too loud,
And I couldn't break free, I wasn't allowed.

So I leave you this echo, this whisper, this cry,
Of a soul that was lost, of a question, why?
Why couldn't I stay, why couldn't I breathe,
In a world that's too harsh, in a life I couldn't weave?

And as you stand in the light of the day,
Remember the ones who faded away,
Not by choice, not by will, but by the hands of time,
By the weight of a world that made them mime.
But know this, as I drift into the night,
I was more than their words, more than their spite,
And though I'm gone, my echo remains,
In the hearts that break, in the tears that stain.

So if you're listening, if you can hear,
Hold on to those who tremble in fear,
And maybe one day, you'll see the light,
In the eyes of a child who fought the fight.

But for now, in the silence, I rest my case,
A voice once strong, now lost in space,
But I leave you with this, a final refrain,
Listen to the whispers of those in pain.

I wasn't always this quiet, you know,
Once had a voice that sang in the flow,
But they told me to hush, to shrink, to hide,
And so I did, till I silently died.

- By Arshan

Part V

Empowerment Tools and Resources

– Chapter 7 – Educational Resources & Guides

This chapter presents a curated list of educational resources and guides on identity and LGBTQIA+ topics that can help me read beyond this book and broaden my understanding.

Books for Personal Development

These books focus on self-acceptance, mental health, personal growth, and navigating identity in a way that empowers LGBTQIA+ individuals and allies.

- "Untamed" by Glennon Doyle – A powerful memoir about breaking free from societal expectations and embracing one's true self.
- "The Velvet Rage: Overcoming the Pain of Growing up Gay in a Straight Man's World" by Alan Downs – A deep exploration of the emotional struggles faced by gay men and how to live authentically.
- "Queer Virtue: What LGBTQ People Know about Life and Love and How It Can Revitalize Christianity" by Rev. Elizabeth M. Edman – A thought-provoking look at how queerness aligns with spiritual and moral growth.
- "The Gifts of Imperfection" by Brené Brown – Encourages self-acceptance and embracing vulnerability as a strength.
- "Self-Compassion: The Proven Power of Being Kind to Yourself" by Dr. Kristin Neff – A guide to replacing self-criticism with self-love and resilience.

- "This Is How It Always Is" by Laurie Frankel – A novel exploring gender identity, family, and acceptance.
- "Real Queer America: LGBT Stories from Red States" by Samantha Allen – A journey through LGBTQIA+ communities in conservative regions, showing resilience and hope.
- "Queerly Beloved: A Love Story across Genders" by Diane and Jacob Anderson-Minshall – A memoir about love, transition, and self-discovery.
- "How to They/Them: A Guide to Non-binary Pronouns and the World of Gender Fluidity" by Stuart Getty – A fun and accessible guide to non-binary identity.
- "The Self-Love Experiment" by Shannon Kaiser – A personal journey towards embracing self-worth and self-care.
- "Daring Greatly" by Brené Brown – Explores how embracing vulnerability can lead to a fulfilling life.
- "You Are Enough: A Book about Inclusion" by Margaret O'Hair and Sofia Sanchez – A beautifully written book about self-acceptance and belonging.
- "Over the Top" by Jonathan Van Ness – A raw and inspiring memoir about overcoming challenges and embracing self-worth.
- "The Queer and Transgender Resilience Workbook" by Anneliese Singh – Practical exercises to build confidence and navigate challenges.
- "Radical Acceptance" by Tara Brach – Teaches mindfulness and self-compassion as a way to overcome self-doubt.

- "Braving the Wilderness" by Brené Brown – Explores the importance of belonging to yourself first.
- "A Guide to Gender: The Social Justice Advocate's Handbook" by Sam Killermann – A valuable resource for understanding gender and identity.
- "You're the Only One I've Told: The Stories behind Abortion" by Meera Shah – Highlights the intersection of gender, identity, and reproductive rights.
- "The Art of Showing Up" by Rachel Wilkerson Miller – A guide to building meaningful relationships and being present for yourself and others.
- "Queerly Autistic: The Ultimate Guide for LGBTQIA+ Autistic Teens" by Erin Ekins – A supportive resource for those navigating both LGBTQIA+ and autistic identities.
- "Beyond Magenta: Transgender Teens Speak Out" by Susan Kuklin – A collection of real-life stories from transgender teens.
- "The Kindness Method" by Shahroo Izadi – A compassionate approach to personal change and self-improvement.
- "Self-Care for the Real World" by Nadia Narain and Katia Narain Phillips – Encourages self-care and mental well-being.

Articles

Here is a curated list of articles covering various aspects of LGBTQIA+ identity, rights, and social issues.

- *The Science of Gender Identity* examines the biology, psychology, and sociology underlying gender identity and its distinction from sex.

- *Coming Out: A Personal and Societal Perspective* examines the process of coming out, its challenges, and ways to support someone coming out.
- *LGBTQIA+ Mental Health: Risks and Resilience* discusses mental health disparities and ways to build emotional well-being within the community.
- *Why Representation Matters in Media* analyzes the impact of LGBTQIA+ visibility in films, television, and literature.
- *Understanding Intersectionality in LGBTQIA+ Advocacy* explains how race, class, gender, and other social factors intersect to influence queer experiences.
- *LGBTQIA+ Rights around the World* provides a comparative analysis of LGBTQIA+ legal protections in different countries.
- *How to Be a Better Ally* provides actionable steps to support LGBTQIA+ individuals in daily life.
- *The Role of Religion in LGBTQIA+ Acceptance* investigates how various religious beliefs interact with LGBTQIA+ identities.
- *The History of Pride: From Stonewall to Today* examines the origins of Pride and its enduring significance.
- *Gender Dysphoria and Medical Transition* explains gender dysphoria and the different transition options available to transgender individuals.

External Resources

There are also many websites, organizations, and helplines that provide support, advocacy, and education.

- The Keshav Suri Foundation (KSF) focuses on embracing, empowering, and mainstreaming the deeply marginalized.
- Glad Foundation focuses on empowerment, career development, and workplace inclusion for LGBTQIA+ individuals.
- The Trevor Project (thetrevorproject.org) provides crisis intervention and suicide prevention services for LGBTQIA+ youth.
- PFLAG (pflag.org) provides support, education, and advocacy for LGBTQIA+ people and their families.
- GLAAD (glaad.org) is a media advocacy organization that promotes fair and accurate LGBTQIA+ representation.
- It Gets Better Project (itgetsbetter.org) does the storytelling and promotes empowerment for LGBTQIA+ youth.
- Trans Lifeline (translifeline.org) is a peer-support hotline run by and for transgender people.
- Stonewall (stonewall.org.uk) is a UK-based LGBTQIA+ rights organization offering educational resources and activism guidance.
- Human Rights Campaign (hrc.org) is an advocacy group working on LGBTQIA+ policy and legal rights.
- National Center for Transgender Equality (transequality.org) engages in policy advocacy and provides resources for transgender rights.

- LGBT Foundation (lgbt.foundation) provides mental health resources, legal support, and community programs.
- OutRight International (outrightinternational.org) is a global organization that advocates for LGBTQIA+ rights worldwide.

Reading List

Here is a list of books that educate, inspire, and provide deeper insights into LGBTQIA+ history, struggles, and personal stories.

- "Gender Queer" by Maia Kobabe – A graphic memoir exploring non-binary identity and self-acceptance.
- "Stonewall: The Definitive Story" by Martin Duberman – A detailed historical account of the Stonewall Riots.
- "Redefining Realness" by Janet Mock – A powerful memoir about growing up as a transgender woman of color.
- "Sissy: A Coming-of-Gender Story" by Jacob Tobia – A humorous and heartfelt story of gender non-conformity.
- "The ABCs of LGBT+" by Ash Hardell – An accessible and informative guide to LGBTQIA+ terminology.
- "Transgender History" by Susan Stryker – A thorough exploration of transgender history in the United States.
- "We Have Always Been Here" by Samra Habib – A memoir about being queer and Muslim.
- "This Book Is Gay" by Juno Dawson – A light-hearted yet educational book on LGBTQIA+ identity.

- "The Gay Revolution" by Lillian Faderman – A history of the LGBTQIA+ rights movement.
- "Beyond the Gender Binary" by Alok Vaid-Menon – Challenges the binary view of gender and offers a fresh perspective.

Tools for Personal Development

Here are some resources and activities to encourage self-acceptance, mental well-being, and advocacy skills.

- LGBTQIA+ Support Groups are online and in-person communities that offer peer support and counseling.
- Mindfulness and Meditation Apps (e.g., Headspace, Calm) help reduce anxiety and improve mental well-being.
- Pronoun Practice Tools (e.g., Practice with Pronouns) provide online exercises to help individuals become accustomed to using different pronouns.
- Coming Out Guides (e.g., PFLAG's Guide to Coming Out) provide strategies and support for coming out safely.
- Self-Reflection Journals are guided journaling prompts to help LGBTQIA+ individuals explore their identity.
- Therapist Directories (e.g., Psychology Today, Inclusive Therapists) help individuals find LGBTQIA+-affirming mental health professionals.
- Social Justice & Advocacy Workshops are online courses and in-person training for LGBTQIA+ activism.
- Legal Aid for LGBTQIA+ Individuals (e.g., Lambda Legal) offers legal guidance and resources for discrimination cases.

- Allyship Training Programs are structured courses teaching effective allyship and advocacy skills.
- Affirmation Exercises are daily self-affirmations designed to boost self-confidence and self-love.

– Chapter 8 –
Allyship & Community Building

Allyship 101

Being an ally to the LGBTQIA+ community is not just a "June job". It means listening, learning, and standing by the community. It means standing up against discrimination and doing your best to make a difference, no matter how small.

What Is Allyship?

There are many aspects to being an Ally.

The first thing you should do, as an ally, is educate yourself on LGBTQIA+ identities, terms, and anything you can get your hands on. It means respecting and supporting the community and releasing biases.

You should stand up against discrimination against the community (intentional or unintentional). Whether it is a harmful joke, bias, systematic injustice, or a throwaway comment, do your best to make the offender understand the impact of their actions.

Allyship needs to start with an examination of self, to better understand the power, privilege, and access available to you as an individual and use that to further help others.

True allyship means using your privilege to challenge oppressive systems, calling out harmful behaviors, and fostering a world where diversity is celebrated, not merely tolerated. It is about learning, listening, and growing.

The Foundation of Allyship: Empathy and Understanding

At the heart of allyship lies **empathy** — the ability to understand and share the feelings of another person. Many

LGBTQIA+ individuals face systemic discrimination, social rejection, and mental health struggles due to societal biases. An ally seeks to understand these experiences without judgment, offering support and solidarity rather than pity.

To cultivate empathy:

- **Listen Actively:** When someone shares their experiences, listen without interrupting or invalidating their feelings.
- **Educate Yourself:** Read books, watch documentaries, and follow LGBTQIA+ activists to learn about their struggles and triumphs.
- **Ask, Don't Assume:** If you do not know something, ask respectfully rather than making assumptions about someone's identity or experiences.

Understanding is key to building meaningful connections and supporting LGBTQIA+ individuals in a way that respects their lived realities.

Dos and Don'ts of Being an Ally

DOs:

- Listen to LGBTQIA+ voices, and learn from their experience and personal knowledge.
- Normalize sharing pronouns and make the area and environment more inclusive and open.
- Avoid using terms like 'Ladies and Gents' or 'Husband/Wife'. Instead, use 'One and All,' or 'Partner.'
- Stand up against homophobic or transphobic remarks or comments.

DON'TS

- Do not make it about you. Being an ally is about the community, not about proving something.
- Do not expose any member. Remember, coming out to a community is the individual's choice, not yours. If they trust you, do not break that trust.
- Allyship does not end with June. Being an ally is not a seasonal trend. It is a yearlong commitment.

Ways to Be an Active Ally

There are many ways to show up as an ally, both in personal and public spaces. Some of the most effective forms of allyship include:

1. Speak Up Against Discrimination

- Call out homophobic, transphobic, or exclusionary language when you hear it—whether in classrooms, workplaces, or at home.
- Advocate for inclusive policies in schools, workplaces, and communities.
- Challenge stereotypes and misinformation whenever you encounter them.

2. Normalize Inclusive Language

- Use correct names and pronouns for individuals, and respect gender identities.
- Add pronouns (he/him, she/her, they/them) in email signatures and social media bios to normalize gender identity awareness.
- Avoid gendered assumptions in conversations—ask "Do you have a partner?" instead of "Do you have a boyfriend/girlfriend?"

3. Support LGBTQIA+ Rights & Representation

- Amplify LGBTQIA+ voices by supporting queer artists, writers, and activists.
- Participate in pride events, workshops, and discussions that promote inclusion.
- Donate to organizations working for LGBTQIA+ rights, particularly those that support queer youth.

4. Create Safe Spaces

- Encourage schools and workplaces to establish gender-neutral restrooms.
- Support the implementation of LGBTQIA+ inclusive education.
- Be a trusted person that LGBTQIA+ individuals can turn to without fear of judgment.

How to be an Ally beyond Pride Month?

- Be supportive of LGBTQIA+ businesses or creators: Explore and use queer-owned brands as a show of support.
- Donate: Donate to LGBTQIA+ organizations.
- Be an advocate: Vote for pro-LGBTQIA+ policies.
- Be an ally in private (as well): Speak for rights even in school, with your family, or at your job.

It is no secret that a little support can go a long way in a situation such as this.

Be an ally. Show your support. Every person counts.

Allyship is a Journey

Allyship is about standing up for equality even when it is uncomfortable, amplifying the voices of those who are marginalized, and continuously working toward a world where everyone, regardless of their gender or sexuality, feels safe and valued.

Every small action counts. Whether it is using inclusive language, educating yourself, or simply offering support, your efforts as an ally contribute to making the world a more accepting and, most importantly, a humane place for us today and for future generations.

Breaking Myths about Allyship

Do you think being an ally means just saying, "I support you?"

No, it is more than that. **Ally is a verb.** So, stand up, speak up and educate yourself.

There are so many myths and so much stigma floating around the concept of being an ally to LGBTQIA+ individuals. Let's clear some of these!

Allyship is a One-Time Act

This is a common misconception that many people hold. Doing one good deed for a community does not make you an automatic ally. Allyship is an ongoing commitment to support and advocate for LGBTQIA+ individuals.

Allies Should Speak for the LGBTQIA+ Community

True allyship is about amplifying LGBTQIA+ voices, not replacing them. We should focus on creating spaces where LGBTQIA+ members can share their experiences, knowledge, and perspectives. It is about speaking with the community, acting as a megaphone, not replacing their voices.

Allyship Is Solely about Individual Actions

While individual actions are important and can bring about change, especially for the individual, systematic change is also crucial. There is no use in changing individual circumstances if the system continues to create more problems than we can solve. This may involve advocating for policy changes, challenging discrimination, promoting diversity, and advocating for rights. Individual actions are important, but systematic change is required for true change.

Allies Should Be Recognized and Praised for Their Efforts

Allyship is not about seeking recognition. It is about doing your part and supporting the LGBTQIA+ community without expecting a reward. It is a service. True allyship is driven by the desire to create positive change, not personal gain. You are considered an ally based on your actions, not through self-proclamation.

Knowing an LGBTQIA+ member means automatic allyship

There is a difference between advocacy and association. You may know a member of the community, but that does not automatically make you an ally. You become an ally through your actions, not through associations.

Put yourself in their shoes. If someone tried to oppress you, judge you for being your true self, would you be disheartened? Would you be hurt? Treat others the same way you would want to be treated in that situation!

Choose empathy. Choose love. Choose to be the person who makes the world a little kinder for someone who just wants to be themselves.

– Chapter 9 –
Interactive Exercises & Activities

Journaling allows us to process our emotions, challenge our biases, gain clarity on our beliefs and get to know ourselves better.

Use these prompts as a guide for self-exploration and to find your *'Astitva.'*

Identity & Self-Discovery

- How would you introduce yourself? Who are you beyond your accomplishments? Explore the aspects of your identity that make you unique.
- What parts of your identity do you feel most connected to? Which aspects of yourself do you fully embrace and absolutely adore yourself for?
- What parts of your identity make you hate yourself? Hate is a strong emotion, and addressing this is a crucial step to accepting yourself.
- Have you ever felt like you do not belong? Reflect on moments when you felt excluded—how did that experience shape you?
- What makes you feel truly seen and understood? Identify what environments or relationships allow you to be your most authentic self.

Personal Growth & Self-Acceptance

- What limiting beliefs do you hold about yourself? How do these beliefs affect your confidence and decision-making?
- When was the last time you stepped out of your comfort zone? What did you learn from that experience?
- What advice would you give to your younger self about self-acceptance? Imagine writing a letter to your past self.
- How do you practise self-love and self-care? What habits help you feel grounded and confident in who you are?
- What are your core values? What values and principles do you live by that are non-negotiable?
- What do you fear the most? Failing? Not reaching your full potential?
- What is one area in your life where you can use more self-discipline?
- What is one habit in your life that is not serving you? Think of bad habits you have already overcome – how did you do that?
- How do you typically deal with negative emotions? Do you have a healthy outlet, or is it more of a coping mechanism?
- Imagine that you are living your dream life right now. Describe your day and activities in detail. What does your day's schedule look like? What can you do to achieve this? How far is your life from the life you have envisioned?

Empathy & Understanding

- When was the last time you made an assumption about someone? How did that assumption affect you and them?
- Have you ever judged someone before getting to know them? What led you to that judgment, and how can you be more open-minded?
- How do you react when someone shares a personal struggle with you? Do you listen with empathy (by putting yourself in their shoes), or do you rush to offer a response or provide solutions?
- What privileges do you have that others may not have? Reflect on all the blessings that you have, which are not widely available to others.

Allyship & Advocacy

- What does being an ally mean to you? Define allyship in your own words and how you practise it in daily life.
- Have you ever spoken up against discrimination? If yes, how did it feel? If not, what stopped you?
- What fears hold you back from advocating for others? Explore any hesitations or discomfort you may have around activism and consider ways to overcome them.
- What steps can you take to create a more inclusive environment in your school, workplace, or community? Identify three concrete actions you can implement to use your privilege and help others around you.

Embrace the adventure of life—step out of your comfort zone and dare to explore the unknown. Every new experience is a chance to learn more about who you truly are. Remember, the most important relationship you will ever have is with yourself. People may come and go, but you will always be with yourself. Accept every part of who you are, even those aspects you might find challenging. Strive to improve based on your core values and principles, but never forget to love yourself first. Self-love is not easily mastered; it must be nurtured from within. Without it, external validation will never fill the void.

Cultivate kindness toward yourself, and let that love shine outwards.

Acknowledgements

As I sit down to write these words, I am still in awe of how far we have come. What started as a mere idea—just a spark—has now grown into something so much bigger than I ever imagined. This journey began in September 2023, in a conversation with Ms. Urmil, where I first voiced my dream of starting an organization dedicated to empowering and educating teenagers. That conversation planted the first seed of what would become Astitva Teens.

From there, I had the privilege of crossing paths with **Mr. Akshay Tyagi**, who became my guide, my mentor, and my unwavering point of contact at every step. And then, through him, I met **Mr. Keshav Suri**, a philanthropist and founder of The Keshav Suri Foundation, a force of inspiration who not only supported me but encouraged me to reach for the stars. I remember how nervous I was before meeting him, unsure of whether someone of his stature would believe in me, in this idea. But he did. And that belief, that encouragement, became a powerful driving force.

I am also incredibly grateful to the **Pride Circle team**, especially **Mahak** and **Vaibhav**, whose unwavering support helped us bring our second event and fundraisers to life. Their guidance ensured that Astitva Teens continued to grow and reach more hearts.

Before all of this, there was another dream—one that felt just as impossible at the time. A panel discussion. Astitva Panel Discussion was new, unfamiliar, and far from easy to organize. But I wanted to do it, and I wanted to do it right. My school, **Pathways School Gurgaon (PSG)**, gave me that chance. They stood behind me, giving me the space and support to bring this initiative to life.

I extend my deepest gratitude to **Captain Rohit Sen Bajaj**, our school director, who listened to my vision and not only approved me to pursue it but also believed in me and supported me every step of the way. **Ms. Dimpu Sharma**, the Middle School Principal, was instrumental in approving the proposal, gathering student and teacher participation, and ensuring the event thrived. **Mr. Rajeev Sharma**, our Deputy Principal, was not just a point of contact—he was a pillar of strength. He helped me sustain Astitva Teens, watched it grow, and in doing so, helped me grow as well.

A special thank you to **Ms. Ritu Pant**, our Instructional Coach for Service Learning. Despite being swamped with countless programs and initiatives, she prioritized Astitva. She was there from the beginning—helping me draft proposals, create engaging content, and manage logistics. More than that, she taught me life lessons I will carry forever. If she hadn't seen potential in this idea, I don't know if I would have had the courage to take it this far. Thank you, ma'am, for believing in me.

And then, there's **Ms. Shweta Khurana**. My form tutor was in 8th grade. My English teacher. The first person to ever grade me as low as she did—and I am glad she challenged me, because it made me strive harder. More than a teacher, she became my constant in a world of change. She saw me through the toughest phases of my teenage years, guiding me, listening to me, and pushing me to be better. Whether it was Astitva Teens or my personal journey, she has been my anchor. Ma'am, no amount of gratitude could ever express how much you mean to me.

To **my team**, you have been there through thick and thin. From organising the Astitva Panel Discussion to shaping this book, you have stood by every initiative, every wild idea I brought to the table. You are Astitva Teens, and thank you for standing by me and this initiative.

And to my **friends**, thank you for your unwavering support. I am deeply grateful for each and every one of you. You have supported in ways I couldn't have imagined.

To **my parents**, there are no words grand enough to capture what you mean to me. **Mom**, you taught me how to read, how to write, how to find my voice. You have been my rock, my safe space, my guiding light. **Dad**, thank you for believing in me when I couldn't believe in myself. You are a founding member of Astitva Teens, and without your wisdom and guidance, none of this would have been possible. You encouraged me to aim high and helped me achieve everything I dreamed of.

Thank you both for being my cook, my chauffeur, my therapist, my Google searches, my everything.

And finally, **to you**—the reader.

Thank you for holding this book in your hands, for reading these words, for becoming a part of this journey. Your contribution will go beyond these pages; it will ripple outward, helping create safer, kinder, more accepting spaces—and, hopefully, a better world.

And so, as we come full circle, I ask you: *What is your Astitva?*

Because the world we dream of—the one where every identity is honoured, every voice is heard, and every person is embraced for who they truly are—it isn't a distant fantasy. It is right here, waiting for us.

So now, as we stand before **the door**—a door that leads to something bigger than ourselves—remember: we are not just passing through. We are holding it open for others. We are shaping a world where everyone belongs.

This is only the beginning.

Welcome home!